G000123116

VENEZUELA

A Guide to the People, Politics and Culture

James Ferguson

The Latin America Bureau is an independent research and publishing organisation. It works to broaden public understanding of issues of human rights and social and economic justice in Latin America and the Caribbean.

First published in the UK in 1994 by Latin America Bureau (Research and Action) Ltd, 1 Amwell Street, London EC1R 1UL

Dutch language edition published by Royal Tropical Institute, Mauritskade 63, 1092 AD Amsterdam, and Novib, The Hague, The Netherlands

© 1994 Royal Tropical Institute/Novib and James Ferguson

© 1994 English Edition Latin America Bureau

A CIP catalogue record for this book is available from the British Library

ISBN 0 906156 92 0

Edited by: Duncan Green
Cover photograph by: Ricardo Bravo
Cover design by: Andy Dark
Design by: Vincent Peters
Cartography by: K. Prins, M. Rieff jr.
Printed by: SSN - Nijmegen, The Netherlands

Trade distribution in the UK by: Central Books, 99 Wallis Road, London E9 5LN
Distribution in North America by: Monthly Review Press, 122 West 27th Street, New York, NY 10001

CONTENTS

Caracas: cars, concrete and carbon
monoxide. The towers of Parque
Central.
(Julio Etchart/Reportage)

INTRODUCTION

The Monday morning of 27 February 1989 started as usual for most of the hundreds of thousands of Venezuelans who live in the shanty towns encircling Caracas. The weekend was over, another eternity of routine stretched ahead before pay-day. Making their way down the precipitous paths and stairways which wind between the hillside shacks, they headed for the nearest main road and the bus which would take them to work in some factory, shop or office.

Venezuelans had voted three months earlier to return Carlos Andrés Pérez to the presidency. He had been in office during the oil boom years of the 1970s when even the poor became a little less poor. In his inaugural speech eleven days ago, he had talked vaguely of economic changes and even sacrifices; 'utopias lead to bankruptcy', he said. But most people hoped that the old Pérez magic would work again, that the good times would return.

As people flagged down buses, the drama began. Bus drivers angrily insisted that they had had to double fares over the weekend because Pérez had doubled the price of petrol. Students were told that their discount cards were no longer valid. The first violence erupted at the Nuevo Circo bus station in the city centre. Rocks and bricks were thrown, roadblocks went up, buses were set on fire.

Within hours Caracas was gripped by insurrection. People streamed down from the slums to help themselves to food, clothes and anything else from the shops whose windows they smashed. Some police and troops tried to intervene. Others actively helped the looters. Fabricio Ojeda, a journalist from *El Nacional,* reported that grateful slum-dwellers passed soldiers presents through the smashed-in shop windows. People careered along the main streets of Caracas, pushing supermarket trolleys crammed with loot or dragging entire beef carcasses from butchers' shops. As news of the *caracazo* reached other towns in Venezuela, similar riots broke out.

Eventually, on Wednesday, a massive military presence retook control of Caracas. By then, many shops and streets were in ruins. The army arrested thousands of people as they swept through the shanty towns searching for stolen goods. In the course of the following week, perhaps 1,500 people died at the hands of the military, although the government admitted to only 287. Soldiers opened fire without warning in poor *barrios,* people who appeared suddenly at windows were shot dead by nervous troops.

The *caracazo* marked the end of Venezuela's oil utopia and the beginning of its current economic crisis. It symbolises the disappearance of 'Saudi Venezuela', the free-spending windfall economy, and the arrival of austerity and structural adjustment. Today Venezuelans look back on that day as both an end and a beginning.

Much has happened since the infamous *27 de febrero*. Venezuela has lost its reputation for political stability and for petro-dollar prosperity. Now the country faces uncertainties in the form of falling oil prices, military unrest and a growing social crisis. The following chapters look at some of these changes and their impact on Venezuelans. They also look at how the country, for all its economic and political woes, remains a vibrant and fascinating mix of people, cultures and landscapes.

I   LAND AND PEOPLE

In Search of El Dorado

Venezuela has always been the prototype of El Dorado. The first Spanish *conquistadores* dreamed of fantastic treasure hidden in its jungles. Later, oil prospectors and companies rushed to the country in search of 'black gold'. Even today, gold miners from Brazil scour the Amazon forests for the find which may make their fortune.

Venezuela enjoys its self-image of grandeur and natural wealth. Each evening before the televison news, Venezuelans are treated to a spectacular aerial panorama of their country's landscapes. To the strains of the national anthem, the film pans across idyllic Caribbean beaches, snow-capped mountains, the huge Orinoco river and the futuristic highrise skyline of the capital, Caracas.

■ Changing Landscapes

Venezuela's landscape is as varied as it is vast. The Andes reach 5,000 metres near the city of Mérida and their peaks are often covered in snow. The 300,000 sq km of the *llanos* or plains, in contrast, are flat, treeless and ideal for cattle ranching. To the East, the expanse of Guayana and the Amazonian territory is dominated by the Orinoco and includes jungle, plains and mountains. Venezuela is also a Caribbean country, with 72 offshore islands, hundreds of kilometres of beaches and growing tourism.

Venezuela's geography boasts many superlatives: it has the world's highest waterfall, Angel Falls, South America's largest lake, Lake Maracaibo, and the longest coastline in the Caribbean. Perhaps most importantly, Venezuela has one of the world's largest deposits of oil, with proven reserves of nearly 63 billion barrels.

The country's varied geography and resources have been key factors in its economic development. In Venezuela's history different regions have played different roles and have risen and fallen in prominence. Most recently, the transition from an agricultural economy to one based on oil and heavy industry has brought about significant changes in how Venezuelans view their land and its resources.

The Coast

Venezuela's first colonial settlements were on the islands of Cubagua and Margarita and then on the coast itself. The impenetrability of much of the country led the early colonists to stay close to the sea, and much of their trade was with the Caribbean island colonies of Cuba and Hispaniola. The huge Orinoco delta was seen as a possible entry into what explorers believed was the fabulous realm of El Dorado, but its heat, humidity and swamps discouraged any permanent settlement.

Most Venezuelans still live in the coastal region and hinterland, where the cities of Maracay, Valencia, Barquisimeto and Maracaibo are centres for agriculture or the oil industry. The first important export commodity, cacao, was grown in the coastal districts and valleys around Caracas. As cacao gave way to coffee in the 19th century as the country's main export, this region's economic importance lessened.

But two modern economic phenomena have revived the coastal region's fortunes. The first is oil, initially discovered in large quantities in Lake Maracaibo, which has transformed the north-western state of Zulia from a sweltering backwater into the country's economic powerhouse. The second is tourism which is gradually changing the face of the 1,500 km coastline. Already seaside towns and resorts like Puerto La Cruz, Choroní and Higuerote have lines of high-rise hotels and beachside bars, while Margarita island attracts charter flights and package tours from Europe and North America.

The Andes

The main spur of the Venezuelan Andes drops into the south-western corner of the country and turns north, cutting off the flat area around Lake Maracaibo to the west and finally levelling off into the Caribbean. Another range runs parallel to the coast, providing the spectacular mountain back-cloth to Caracas.

Less dramatic than the Andes of Peru or Bolivia, Venezuela's part of the range is nonetheless impressive, with its mixture of windswept highlands, green valleys and glaciers. This part of the country had its economic hey-day in the 1830s when coffee enjoyed an export boom through European traders. The valleys around Mérida and San Cristóbal became coffee plantations, creating enormous wealth for local landowners.

Even before then, however, the Andean region had been the most agri-culturally developed, with evidence of sophisticated cultivation techniques used by pre-Columbian indigenous communities.

Today, the region is still agriculturally productive, but economically insignificant compared to other oil-rich parts of the country. The climate and scenery attract many visitors, and Mérida is an important university and tourist town, but the days of Andean supremacy are long gone.

The llanos

The vast expanse of plains known as the *llanos* accounts for about one third of Venezuelan territory but contains probably less than 10 per cent of its human population. People are outnumbered by cattle, of which there are approximately five million. With the exception of occasional hillocks (*mesas*) and clumps of palm trees, the region is relentlessly flat. Meandering rivers are the habitat for an extraordinary range of wildlife, including the ferocious piranha fish. Each year from May to November torrential rains flood the plains, forcing the cowboys to drive the cattle up onto the *mesas*. Eventually the herds are driven to the fertile valleys near Valencia and Maracay to be fattened for slaughter.

There are few towns in the *llanos* and roads are poor. In the 19th century the state of Guárica was briefly one of the richest and most populated regions of Venezuela, attracting migrants and capital with its huge ranches. But Venezuela's livestock industry could not compete with the modernised, refrigerated export businesses of Argentina and Uruguay and the *llanos* reverted to their state of wilderness. Until recently the region was the most undeveloped and neglected in Venezuela. The government is now investing in cotton and rice production in parts of the *llanos,* while the flat plains continue as home to millions of cattle.

Guayana

The huge area known as Guayana covers 45 per cent of Venezuela and contains some of its richest resources and most beautiful scenery. The region has always fascinated explorers and adventurers and was for a long time reputed to contain the legendary kingdom of El Dorado. In the late 19th century there was a shortlived gold rush at El Callao, and since then miners have scoured rocks and rivers in search of a quick fortune. In September 1993 a Canadian mining company announced that it had identified reserves of gold totalling 150 tonnes in Bolívar State.

Nowadays most of Guayana's wealth lies in its massive petrochemical, steel and aluminium plants which are powered by hydroelectricity from the Caroní river. Since the 1960s the new town of Ciudad Guayana has grown from a small provincial outpost to a burgeoning city of more than 600,000 people.

The unique scenery of the Guayana region has encouraged a small but growing tourist industry in this otherwise remote area. The chief attraction is the extraordinary Angel Falls, the 979 metre high waterfall named after the US pilot, Jimmy Angel, who crash-landed his light aircraft there in 1937. The 'Gran Sabana', a vast valley dotted with some 100 flat-topped mountains *(tepuis)* is reputed to have inspired Sir Arthur Conan Doyle's *The Lost World* and more recently featured in the spectacular special effects of *Jurassic Park*. An exotic landscape of rivers, rapids, lagoons and forest appeals to a growing number of environmentally-conscious tourists who stay at the jungle resort of Canaima.

Angel Falls.
(Edward Paine/Last Frontiers)

Angel Falls

The world's highest waterfall flows breathtakingly over the rim of the Auyantepui ('devil mountain'), one of the **Gran Sabana**'s flat-topped mountains. Fifteen times higher than **Niagara**, the falls are named after a US pilot and adventurer, **Jimmy Angel**, who came across them in 1937. Angel had already taken part in a gold-panning expedition in the area, landing his aircraft on top of a *tepui* accompanied by a mysterious prospector whom he had met in a **Panama City** bar. Together they had returned with forty pounds of gold. Determined to find his own **El Dorado** again, **Angel** flew back to the **Gran Sabana** and this time crash-landed on top of **Auyantepui**.

The second trip produced no gold, but Angel chanced upon the enormous waterfall which had hitherto remained unknown in modern Venezuela. After a trek of eleven days, he returned with stories of his extraordinary discovery. It was not until 1949 that an overland expedition verified Angel's claim. His aircraft now stands outside the small local airport at Ciudad Bolívar, having been dug out of the muddy mountain-top in 1970. Angel died in a plane crash in Panama in 1956, poor, unknown and over-fond of whisky.

■ The Melting Pot

Venezuela prides itself on being the melting pot of South America. Its 20 million people include indigenous Indians, Europeans, Africans and migrants from other Latin American and Caribbean countries. Racism, it is claimed, is unknown in a *café con leche* (coffee with milk) culture. As Arturo Uslar Pietri, the country's most venerated intellectual, has written, 'In Venezuela there are neither whites nor blacks, neither *mestizos* nor Indians. There are only Venezuelans.'

The mixture of Americans, Africans and Europeans has given Venezuela a rich variety of social and cultural forms. The country contains some of South America's remotest indigenous communities which until recently have avoided contact with modern civilisation. It is also home to a large population of immigrants from Europe who arrived in the 1950s and settled in Caracas and other cities. Slavery has also left its mark on Venezuela, with a distinctive Afro-Venezuelan culture on the Caribbean coast.

Together, and with the addition of recent immigrants from Colombia and Guyana, these cultures have formed a mixed population very different from the original hierarchical colonial society. Under Spanish rule the white elite occupied the top of the social pyramid, the mixed-race *pardos* the middle, and blacks and Indians the lowest positions. Today, 69 per cent of Venezuelans define themselves as mixed-race, 20 per cent as white, 9 per cent as black and 2 per cent as Indian.

But despite its claims to racial democracy, Venezuela is still a highly unequal society, in which wealth and power tend to lie in the hands of a white elite. In the expensive hotels and clubs of Caracas there are few black faces other than those of the staff. At the same time, the capital's shanty towns and the poor rural villages contain a large proportion of darker-skinned Venezuelans.

The First Venezuelans

On a dusty, litter-strewn roadside in the modern jungle city of Ciudad Guayana a group of Indian women and children stand listlessly waiting for the traffic lights to turn red. The impatient motorists mostly ignore their

The melting pot: Venezuela's
mixed population.
(Paddy Donnelly)

outstretched hands at the car windows, unwilling to let the sweltering heat
outside ruin their air-conditioned comfort.

The indigenous people of Venezuela are among the country's poorest
and most marginalised communities. Some are forced to come and beg in
the towns and cities between the Orinoco river and the Brazilian border or
have become dependent on the handouts of missionaries. Others, remaining
in their traditional Amazonian lands, are vulnerable to attacks from *garimpeiros,* miners and gold prospectors who often come from Brazil.

The Yanomami, who number about 14,000, face the threat of violence
and disease as well as the poisoning of rivers and streams by miners'
mercury. They complain that the government has defined their ancestral
lands as 'areas under special administrative rule' or national parks in order
to stop them from using their natural resources.

In July 1993, at least 13 Yanomami, including six children were murdered by *garimpeiros* in the remote border region. The miners, it is thought,
had come to take revenge on the community after two of their fellow
workers had been killed in a dispute with some Yanomami, five of whom
were killed on that occasion.

But not all Venezuela's Indians are victims. Numbered between 200,000
and 315,000, a large proportion live in and around the Sinamaica lagoon,
45 kilometres north of Maracaibo and close to the Colombian border. Here,
the largest indigenous group, the Guajiras, have preserved their language
and cultural traditions while prospering from cattle raising and handicrafts
for tourists. During the 1960s and 1970s they were also reputed to have
done well from exporting Colombian marijuana to the us.

Guajira women in Maracaibo.
(Meredith Davenport)

Conquest

Today, according to the National Indian Council of Venezuela (CONIVE), there are 27 linguistically and culturally distinct indigenous groups in the country. History does not record how many people were living in the area when Christopher Columbus first reached the gulf of Paria in August 1498, but estimates have suggested 350,000, divided into many communities. A second Spanish expedition the following year, led by Alonso de Ojeda, made its way into Lake Maracaibo where it came across groups of Indian huts built upon stilts in the shallows. Perhaps sarcastically, the explorers likened the lakeside villages to the canals of Venice, and named the territory Venezuela or 'little Venice'.

The indigenous people whom Columbus and his followers first encountered on the Caribbean coast were just part of a much bigger population which covered much of present-day Venezuela. There were nomadic groups, living from fishing and hunting, around the coast, in the central plains and in the vast forests. The most developed agriculture and trading, however, were to be found in the Andes, although these communities were small and unsophisticated in comparison to the Incas or Aztecs.

But while the great civilisations of Peru and Mexico gave way easily to the *conquistadores*, Venezuela's indigenous people resisted long and hard. The Spanish colonists' first attempts to establish towns and trading routes met with fierce opposition.

The cruelty of the colonists in enslaving Indians to dive for pearls worsened hostilities. In the end, it was disease, principally smallpox, which defeated the indigenous peoples; in 1580 an epidemic in the Caracas valley killed an estimated two-thirds of the local Indian population.

Missionaries were also instrumental in pacifying indigenous communities, and nomadic peoples were often forced into supervised settlements. Others were even less fortunate and were subjected to the *encomienda* system, a form of forced labour. As Venezuela's colonial system developed, its first inhabitants were pushed aside, destroyed or forced to survive in the country's most inaccessible regions.

The Fight for Land

The struggle for land and legal land titles is the main issue now affecting Venezuela's Indian population. CONIVE claims that 83 per cent of indigenous communities lack title deeds to their own lands, making them vulnerable to harassment from companies, wildcat miners and ranchers. Communities around Lake Maracaibo have gradually seen their territories taken over by oil companies, while the Cuiva people have faced violence from cattle barons in the Apure region.

Disease also continues to take its toll. Indian communities suffer disproportionately from dysentery, tuberculosis, malaria and, more recently, cholera. Experts blame a lack of primary healthcare as well as poverty and abandonment of traditional medicine. Despite the Venezuelan constitution's commitment to bilingual education, indigenous groups receive little special assistance and their culture is generally ignored or derided by the majority of Venezuelans. The first census of Venezuela's indigenous population in 1992 found that 40 per cent of Indian workers earned less than a third of the statutory minimum wage and that 65 per cent of communities had no access to schools.

Despite five centuries of marginalisation, Venezuela's Indians are now reviving their tradition of resistance and have made some important advances. During the 1970s indigenous groups became more active politically, leading in 1989 to the first national indigenous congress and the founding of CONIVE, made up of twenty indigenous organisations from around the country.

Because of growing pressure from CONIVE and international agencies, the Venezuelan government announced in 1991 that it would set aside 83,000 sq km as permanent territory for the Yanomami. Even so, doubts remain as to whether the authorities are willing or able to protect this territory from outside interests.

European Migrants

In early 1992 the Venezuelan government launched an immigration programme, aimed at encouraging 50,000 east Europeans to the country over a five-year period. The successful applicants, said the minister of planning, should have qualifications and skills of interest to private Venezuelan companies. In return, the government would provide airline tickets and a cash relocation package.

Colonisation

European settlement in Venezuela was initially much slower and more uneven than in other parts of the Spanish empire. The early colony was poor and prone to violence and disease. The first *conquistadores* set off on illusory and often suicidal adventures down the Orinoco river to find the mythical El Dorado. Others were only interested in capturing Indians as slaves for the Caribbean colonies of Hispaniola and Cuba.

Venezuela even underwent a twenty-year period of German colonisation from 1528, when the Spanish monarchy ceded the entire territory to the German banking house of Welser, to which it was heavily indebted. The Welsers, obsessed by the mirage of El Dorado, mounted a series of ruthless and futile expeditions into the interior before abandoning their quest and their lease on Venezuela.

Gradually the colonial process gathered impetus, and Europeans moved inland from the islands of Cubagua and Margarita and the coastal settlements of Cumaná and Coro. The founding in 1545 of El Tocuyo near present-day Barquisimeto marked the beginning of colonial development based more on agriculture and settlement than gold prospecting and slaving. In due course the Spanish conquered the rich agricultural regions of the Caracas and Aragua valleys, where they established ranches and cacao plantations.

But despite its agricultural potential, Venezuela remained on the periphery of the Spanish empire and immigrants were less keen to settle there than in the richer colonies of Mexico or Peru. Settlement was an uneven and piecemeal process, with rival centres to Caracas established in Mérida, Maracaibo and Cumaná.

Tensions with Spain were also a disincentive to European migration, especially when the Spanish crown granted a trade monopoly to a Basque consortium, the Compañía Guipuzcoana, thereby preventing the local elite from trading on the world market. An extended cacao boom from 1750 to the beginning of the 19th century went some way to attracting new colonists, but this was wiped out in the bloodshed of the wars of independence.

The century following Venezuela's violent break with Spain was one of continual turbulence. Even so, migration began to increase slowly, particularly encouraged by those governments which believed in the 'superiority' of

European settlers. In the late 19th century, the dictator Antonio Guzmán Blanco brought several thousand workers from the Canary Islands, while fifty years earlier a community of Germans settled close to Caracas in Colonia Tovar. Today the community, with its Bavarian-style restaurants and souvenir shops, is a popular place for Sunday outings from the capital.

Promised Land

The real rush of European migration only occurred in the 1940s and 1950s with the consolidation of Venezuela's oil-based economy. Growing prosperity and employment prospects in the new industries acted as a magnet to thousands of Europeans left displaced and destitute after the Second World War. The Venezuelan government tried to attract recruits into agriculture with promises of land and credit, but most recent migrants preferred to live in the cities and particularly in Caracas.

The main influx arrived during the mid-1950s in response to immigration programmes pursued by the military dictatorship of General Marcos Pérez Jiménez. Perceiving large-scale European immigration as a central part of his modernisation plans, Pérez Jiménez succeeded in attracting almost half a million migrants - Italians, Spanish and Portuguese - to Venezuela. In the midst of a massive programme of urban redevelopment many of them found work in Caracas in construction, transport and commerce. These newcomers had a much bigger impact in the capital city than elsewhere. A huge number of European restaurants, shops and clubs sprang up, transforming Caracas from a quaint colonial outpost into a thriving, cosmopolitan and politically volatile city.

Afro-Venezuela

Blacks make up perhaps 9 per cent of Venezuela's population. They are concentrated primarily on the Caribbean coast and in villages near Lake Maracaibo, although there is a significant black presence in Caracas. Some Afro-Venezuelans are the descendants of the slaves imported during the 17th and 18th centuries to work on the cacao plantations. There were an estimated 60,000 black slaves in 1810 out of a total population of 900,000 and most were put to work in the coastal region. According to legend, some were thrown overboard as sickly and worthless by slaveship owners as they approached the nearby Dutch colonies of Aruba, Bonaire and Curaçao and managed to swim ashore.

Most slaves came via the Spanish Caribbean colonies of Cuba and Santo Domingo. As well as working in the fields, they were used as domestic servants and urban artisans. Eighteenth-century visitors to Venezuela reported that African slaves were an important status symbol among the white elite, and that wealthy families competed to have the largest retinue of slaves processing with them to Sunday mass.

The wars of independence and ensuing conflicts effectively destroyed Venezuelan slavery, as many blacks were recruited into differing armed forces. The elite also feared slave rebellions and realised that wage labour was economically more viable than slavery. Abolition was finally declared in 1854, but by then most blacks were already free.

Another generation of blacks came to Venezuela after oil was discovered. Migrants from the English- and Dutch-speaking Caribbean were employed in the oilfields of Maracaibo and other areas. This movement was repeated in the 1970s when Venezuela's spectacular oil boom attracted workers from Guyana and Trinidad. Guyanese East Indians still make up an important community in Bolívar State, where they work as self-employed builders and informal vendors.

A Racial Democracy?

The issue of race and racism is controversial in contemporary Venezuela. In theory, the constitution forbids discrimination of any sort and many Venezuelans are proud that the country has never had a history of segregation like that in the US or Cuba. There is certainly some social mobility in modern Venezuela, and several Afro-Venezuelans have risen to high positions in professions, politics and government. But these are exceptional cases, and most black Venezuelans work in poorly paid agricultural or domestic jobs.

Colombians

Today's scapegoats are the Colombians. They are blamed for all manner of social ills, from unemployment and crime to drugs and disease. According to many *Caraqueños*, the grim shanty towns which cling to the hillsides around the capital are full of illegal Colombian immigrants. Colombians form the largest Latin American migrant group, but there are also significant communities from Peru and Ecuador.

Most Colombians came to Venezuela in the 1970s at the height of the oil boom. Wages and conditions were better than at home, and money could easily be sent back to families left behind. Often entire families migrated, women finding low-paid factory jobs or domestic work in Venezuelan homes. Generally, Colombians did the work that Venezuelans preferred to avoid in seasonal agriculture, textile factories and construction. Many still work in the informal sector as *buhoneros* (street vendors) and are regularly harassed by the authorities. Some Venezuelans blame Colombian migrants for lowering wage levels and increasing unemployment.

There are no reliable figures for the numbers of illegal Colombian migrants in Venezuela today, but a popular estimate puts the figure at one million or 5 per cent of the population. In the mid-1970s perhaps 100,000 people crossed the border each year, but this flow dried up in the 1980s and many have since returned home.

Anti-Colombian feeling has surfaced in recent years as Venezuela's economic situation has worsened. Legislation has obliged companies to ensure that at least 90 per cent of their workforce are Venezuelan citizens, thereby preventing the use of cheaper Colombian labour. There has also been controversy over a scheme to register all children born in Venezuela as Venezuelan nationals.

A Young Nation

Caracas has the feel of a young city. From the expensive downtown shopping centres to the ramshackle hillside shanty towns, the overwhelming image is of youth. The statistics support the impression. No fewer than 53 per cent of the population is aged under 20, while only 3.1 per cent is over 65 years of age.

This demographic imbalance stems from the population boom in the 1970s which coincided with that period's oil-fuelled economic bonanza. Declining child mortality rates also helped to push up the numbers of young.

Youth presents both problems and opportunities for Venezuela. As a creaking education system strains under the weight of so many young people and government cutbacks, the threat of social unrest is ever-present. The 'austerity riots' of 1989 as well as subsequent episodes of looting and rioting have shown that widespread poverty and disillusionment exist among large sectors of the young. Crime and drugs are huge problems in Venezuelan cities, particularly in Caracas' shanty towns.

On the other hand, one of Venezuela's most valuable resources is its 'human capital'. In the boom years of the 1970s and 1980s vast sums of money were spent on education, creating a highly qualified workforce of engineers and other professionals. The country's future depends to a large extent on whether continued investment in education and training will enable young Venezuelans to have a stake in tomorrow's economy and society.

2   POLITICAL SYSTEM

Parties, Patronage and Power

In the early hours of 6 December 1993, the avuncular figure of 77-year-old Rafael Caldera appeared at his election headquarters and promised his celebrating supporters *alegría* (joy) in years to come. After three years of what most Venezuelans agree was the country's worst ever crisis, the promise was attractive.

Joyful or not, Caldera's victory hardly suggested a new beginning. The veteran politician had founded the Christian Democratic COPEI party in 1946, had been its president between 1970 and 1974 and had stood for the presidency no fewer than five other times. Many older Venezuelans associated Caldera with the boom years of the early 1970s when high oil revenues were paying for ambitious social spending.

But Caldera's victory did represent something new. For the first time since 1958, the two-party system, in which COPEI and Acción Democrática (AD) have shared or alternated in power, failed to provide the President. Caldera, who stood as the candidate of a motley collection of 17 small parties, the *Convergencia* (baptised the 'cockroach coalition' by the Venezuelan media), had abandoned his own party and upset the political system.

It was not just Caldera's win which sent a shock through the country's powerful political class. Fourth in the polls, but gaining 22 per cent of the vote, was Andrés Velásquez, candidate of the left-wing Causa R ('Radical Cause') and a former SIDOR worker and union leader from Ciudad Guayana. Virtually unknown outside its Guayana power base until local election wins in 1992, Causa R has suddenly and dramatically sprung to prominence.

From a combined election tally of 96 per cent in 1988, AD and COPEI could barely manage 46 per cent of the presidential vote. With an abstention rate of 42 per cent, the figures confirmed that the electorate had rejected the traditional parties. The vote for Congress also showed surprising support for new and alternative parties. Here, however, the two traditional parties maintained significant numbers of seats (only by ballot-rigging and other fraud, alleged Causa R).

■ The End of an Era?

The 1993 election result was the culmination of a long crisis for the old political order. In the preceding eighteen months, two abortive military coups had rocked the country's reputation for stability. The incumbent AD president, Carlos Andrés Pérez, had been impeached on charges of corrup-

Rafael Caldera's victory rally,
December 1993.
(Meredith Davenport)

tion, removed from office, and was awaiting trial. In the wake of the February 1989 *caracazo,* continual strikes, demonstrations, terrorism and rumours of further military intervention had added to the atmosphere of crisis. As a lame-duck interim presidency, headed by Ramón José Velásquez, steered Venezuela towards the elections, many began to look towards Caldera as a saviour.

Caldera's election platform was as mixed as the *Convergencia* which supported him. Backed by the Partido Comunista de Venezuela (PCV, Venezuelan Communist Party) and groups from the extreme left and right as well as the Movimiento al Socialismo (MAS, Movement Towards Socialism), he promised a populist programme of social spending and to eradicate corruption from Venezuelan society.

Not surprisingly, the anti-corruption message of both Caldera and Velásquez proved popular with Venezuelan voters, tired of scandal among the political elite. Also popular were promises not to raise the price of petrol and to control food prices. But it was above all a negative vote, a vote against Pérez, AD and the party system, which took Caldera back to the presidency after twenty years.

Punto Fijo

The modern Venezuelan party system began on 31 October 1958 when Caldera, together with Rómulo Betancourt, the leader of Acción Democrática, and other politicians and business leaders signed the so-called Pact of Punto Fijo. This agreement, named after Caldera's residence, stated that AD and COPEI would share power, irrespective of who won the forthcoming elections in December that year.

Venezuela was just emerging from the dictatorship of General Marcos Pérez Jiménez, and the party leaders were determined to establish a solid partnership against military interventionism and the rapidly growing Venezuelan Communist Party. COPEI could offer AD the important support of the Church and sections of conservative opinion; in return, AD would allow COPEI to participate in government.

In the election, Betancourt won 49 per cent and Caldera only 16 per cent. Honouring the agreement, AD and COPEI governed together and shared power until 1968, when the two parties adopted a more adversarial relationship. Venezuela's constitution, which came into force in 1961, reinforced this concept of political consensus.

Lessons of the trienio

The Pact was a response to the bitter experience of AD's first and brief period in office from 1945 to 1948. Ironically, it was a military coup which put the party in power, when officers, disgruntled with corruption, conspired with AD to overthrow the government of Isaías Medina Angarita and usher in fresh elections. There is still controversy today concerning AD's role in the coup, and opponents claim that the party's involvement discredited its democratic credentials.

AD won the elections and for a three-year period known as the *trienio*, introduced an ambitious series of economic and social reforms. With Rómulo Gallegos as President, the government introduced universal suffrage and increased spending on health and education, funded by rising oil revenues. Political mobilisation in parties, unions and peasant organisations, was intense. AD saw itself as the *partido único*, the natural single party of government, overseeing a social-democratic revolution.

As a result, open conflict broke out between AD and COPEI, especially in the Andes, where rival party supporters clashed violently. The Church, dismayed by the AD government's emphasis on secular state education, also openly attacked the regime. Finally, social unrest and inter-party conflict reached such a pitch that the military again stepped in. Led by Pérez Jiménez, the armed forces took power in November 1948, starting a ten-year period of exceptional corruption and repression.

The Pact of Punto Fijo was designed to prevent party conflicts and sectarianism from provoking another coup and to ensure that neither party would use extra-constitutional means (such as plotting with the army) against its opponent. According to Betancourt, 'inter-party discord was kept to a minimum, and in this way leaders revealed that they had learned the harsh lesson which despotism had taught to all Venezuelans.'

■ The Traditional Parties

Acción Democrática

Until the 1993 election debacle, AD was the best organised, most powerful party in Venezuela. Its social-democratic roots go back to the dictatorship of Juan Vicente Gómez in the 1920s, when its founder members agitated for democratic reforms. The party was officially founded in 1941 by the so-called 'generation of 1928' which included leaders such as Betancourt and the novelist Rómulo Gallegos. Since 1958, AD has won five of the country's eight presidential elections. The party claims a membership of nearly two million.

AD has always presented itself as reformist and nationalist. While Marxism played a part in its early ideology, it has always been strongly anti-communist and based on *policlasista* (multi-class) support. Its successful nationalisation of the oil industry in 1976 reinforced this image, and the party claims to have brought about significant land reform and improvements in workers' rights. Over the years, however, a number of left-wing factions have split from the party, impatient with its lack of radicalism. The Confederación de Trabajadores de Venezuela (CTV, Confederation of Venezuelan Workers), the country's biggest trade union, is affiliated to AD. The party is Latin America's foremost member of the Socialist International.

COPEI

COPEI (the acronym stands for Organising Committee for Independent Electoral Policy) was founded in 1946 by Caldera, a lawyer and prominent Catholic, as a conservative alternative to AD. Its early doctrines reflected its Cold War origins, and Caldera was known to be militantly anti-communist. The party's first power bases were in the more conservative Andes, but today it has a presence throughout the country. Over the years, COPEI has lost its overtly religious identity but remains part of the Christian Democrat International. Today, COPEI claims more than 1.5 million members. It has provided only two presidents since 1958.

In theory, COPEI stands for a more conservative, pro-business outlook than AD. In practice, however, *copeyano* presidents Caldera and Herrera Campins (1979-84) spent heavily on public projects and did little to reduce the role of the state in the Venezuelan economy. In the December 1993 election campaign, the COPEI candidate, Oswaldo Alvarez Paz, weakened by the split with Caldera, performed badly.

The Spoils System

Until the 1993 election upset, the two traditional parties shared or alternated in power in a system which was based on sharing the spoils. With the state the main beneficiary of Venezuela's oil wealth (either through rent and taxes paid by foreign companies or through taxing PDVSA), political power meant access to that wealth. Political parties were vehicles for various groups to distribute the state's resources in the form of public spending, employment and different forms of subsidies.

Oil money bought political stability and a form of social consensus. Parties could reward poor neighbourhoods for their electoral support by providing drinking water, a health clinic or a sports field. The poor grew to expect their small share of the wealth in the form of subsidised basic foods and medicines and other perks. The middle classes came to rely on jobs in the state sector and access for their children to education. The rich maintained their life styles through their relationship, political or economic, with the state and the ruling party.

The 35-year period of Venezuelan two-party democracy was based on control and cooption. As most Venezuelans had some stake, however small, in the system, there was much less social conflict than in other Latin American countries. A brief and unsuccessful guerrilla campaign in the early 1960s failed to win support among the peasantry. Regular elections, peaceful transfers of power and the co-existence enshrined in the Pact of Punto Fijo underpinned the distribution of resources. The system could work for as long as the oil wealth kept flowing. When it slowed down and Venezuela faced economic crisis and austerity, it began to falter.

Partidocrácia

Both AD and COPEI are mass membership parties, with a complex structure of regional branches, committees and leaders. A survey in 1985 concluded that as many as 30 per cent of Venezuelans belonged to a political party, a very high figure considering the low average age of the population.

Activism has always carried its own rewards when the party in question has power, providing jobs, promotion and status for its followers. According to the sociologist Domingo Alberto Rangel: 'The activists who organise or attend assemblies and undertake other routine tasks for the organisation reap the benefits of power...They are peasants who obtain credits from the Agricultural Bank or land from the National Agrarian Institute, barrio residents who are able to get an apartment from INAVI [the housing agency], those who get work in state industries, and middle-class professionals who find themselves on the list of appointments to jobs in the Administration.'

Party politics affect all aspects of Venezuelan life. Control of trade unions, professional societies, university faculties, student associations and neighbourhood organisations is decided by election of party candidates. This pervasive influence has led to the term *partidocrácia*, in which the party supplants the *demos* or people themselves. In this system the party has various different functions: political movement, social club and employment office.

The system inevitably encourages patronage and corruption at every level of society. At the top, businesses have supported a particular party in return for the promise of government contracts and protection against cheaper imports. At the bottom, party membership can make everyday life easier if an individual needs a favour from a local government officer or special treatment in court.

The Power Brokers

At the centre of the system stand the party bosses, known in Venezuela as the *cogollos* (the nuclei or, more graphically, the hearts of the lettuce). They exert great power, both locally and nationally, and are instrumental in maintaining the parties' cohesion and discipline. Some are well-known politicians, such as ministers, senators or state governors who have their own resources and power of patronage. Others are the more faceless bureaucrats who make up national executives and regional committees.

Until recently, the Venezuelan voting system involved a closed list for legislative elections, in which electors chose party slates rather than individuals. This allowed the *cogollos* to select and deselect party activists and functionaries for places in Congress without the voters even knowing their names. As a result, it was almost impossible for a member of Congress to be voted out of office. Reforms carried out by the second Pérez administration introduced more direct democracy, but the influence of the party power brokers remains enormous.

Despite the efforts of the *cogollos,* the two parties have sometimes split between competing leaders and cliques. In 1968, for instance, Caldera won his first term in office with 27 per cent of the vote because AD had suffered a damaging split, with many activists leaving to form the left-wing Movimiento Electoral del Pueblo (MEP, People's Electoral Movement). In 1988 Caldera failed to win the COPEI nomination which went to Eduardo Fernández and refused to campaign for him. Struggles between 'pre-candidates' have often led to exchanges of insults and occasionally to violence between rival supporters.

While parties are all important, personality plays a significant part in Venezuelan politics. Leaders such as Caldera, Pérez and Fernández (*'el tigre'*) have all cultivated an aura of charisma, and elections tend to be fought on personal as much as ideological issues.

◼ Caudillos

The cult of the strong leader within the party system is to some extent a continuation of the earlier Venezuelan tradition of militarism and dictatorship. The *caudillo* or strongman was a permanent feature of the country's chaotic 19th-century history and lasted well into the 20th century. Until the 1940s, parties were almost non-existent and were simply vehicles for local leaders with political ambitions. The violent and fragmented nature of 19th-century Venezuelan life produced a legion of *caudillos* who led their mercenary armies into innumerable wars. Debatably the first, and the most important, *caudillo* was Simón Bolívar, the 'liberator' of Venezuela and today its national icon.

Independence and civil war

The ten-year independence struggle spearheaded by Bolívar and his army removed Spanish rule but ravaged Venezuela's economy and infrastructure. The first independence movement, encouraged by Spain's occupation by France, emerged in 1811 but was savagely repressed by the colonial authorities. A military campaign resulted in the republicans capturing Caracas, but they were defeated again, overwhelmed by the ferocity of the *llanero* horsemen who had sided with the Spanish Crown. When Bolívar won the *llaneros* over to his side with the promise of land, the balance of forces changed. With the support of the *llanero* strongman, José Antonio Páez, the republicans triumphed and finally routed the Spanish in 1821.

Perhaps as many as 150,000 died in the independence war. The cocoa industry was destroyed, and entire towns and villages in ruins. With Bolívar's fall from power and the abandonment of *Gran Colombia*, Venezuela lost its central authority and degenerated into banditry and regional conflicts. A series of *caudillos* equipped and led their own peasant armies.

Between 1830 and 1888, there were 730 armed conflicts and 26 full-scale insurrections in Venezuela. The apogee of the political violence was the Federal War of 1858-63, in which the Liberal and Conservative parties (in reality, groupings of *caudillos)* fought over whether Venezuela should have a federal constitution or be ruled directly from Caracas. While thousands died each year in violence, the economy declined spectacularly. In 1902 Venezuela's unpaid debts led to a naval blockade and bombardment by British, French, German and Italian warships. Foreign companies also meddled openly in the country's politics, supporting one *caudillo* against another in return for economic favours.

The tyrant of the Andes

A sort of peace arrived only with the 27-year dictatorship of Juan Vicente Gómez. The military leader from Táchira defeated a number of rival *caudillos* and formed a modern, centralised army before taking power himself.

Gómez's rule was absolute and ruthless. Critics and opponents faced imprisonment, torture, murder or exile. On one occasion, the dictator deliberately spread a rumour that he had died in order to see – and punish – those who dared to celebrate. He ran the country like his personal *hacienda,* and popular legend has it that he fathered some 150 children. From his cattle ranch in Maracay, Gómez controlled a clique of family and friends with a wider network of informers and secret agents. According to his enemies, he had plundered US$400 million from the treasury by the time of his death.

Bolívar liberates the slaves:
ceiling in museum, Caracas.
(Paddy Donnelly)

The Liberator

Visitors to Venezuela arrive at the Simón Bolívar International Airport in Caracas. There, they change their money into *bolívares,* the national currency. In Caracas they will probably notice that the capital's main square and major thoroughfare are named after Bolívar, as are squares, streets, universities and hospitals throughout the country. There is Bolívar state, a city named Ciudad Bolívar and a mountain peak called Pico Bolívar. Statues, books, soap operas and songs celebrate the Liberator. It is an offence to appear improperly dressed in the capital's Plaza Bolívar as this is interpreted as disrespect to the square's equestrian statue.

The man who was to lead Venezuela to independence from Spain was born in 1783, the heir to a wealthy *gran cacao* family. A period in Europe intro-

Latin America Bureau

Research and action on Latin America and the Caribbean

TO: 1 Amwell Street, London EC1R 1UL
Telephone 071-278 2829

WRITE FOR A <u>FREE</u> 20-page CATALOGUE

Please send me a free catalogue of Latin America Bureau books. I am interested in books on (please tick box/es):

☐ Central America

☐ South America

☐ The Caribbean

Title of book in which you found this catalogue request slip:

_____

NAME ....

ADDRESS ....

....

duced him to revolutionary and republican ideas which he combined with the local elite's resentment against Spain and colonial control. Unlike most of the elite, however, Bolívar had a vision of a progressive and egalitarian society, dominated by a strong central state. The vision extended to the concept of *Gran Colombia,* his design for a united federation of modern Venezuela, Colombia and Ecuador.

Bolívar's commitment to the abolition of slavery and the distribution of land to the poor won him the support of a large and well organised army which finally defeated the Spanish at Carabobo in 1821. He then set off to play a key role in the independence struggles of Peru and Bolivia. His military prowess became legendary, yet his brief period as President of the Venezuelan-Colombian federation was less happy.

Eventually, *Gran Colombia* disintegrated into its national parts, and Bolívar lost political and military power to his lieutenant, José Antonio Páez. His last years were full of disillusionment and he died in Colombia in 1830, having made the famous pronouncement: 'America is ungovernable. He who serves a revolution ploughs the sea.' In The General in His Labyrinth, Gabriel García Márquez depicts the dying Bolívar as afflicted by 'the melancholic certainty that he would die in his bed, poor and naked and without the consolation of public gratitude.'

From dictatorship to democracy

The end of the Gómez regime prompted the return to Venezuela of thousands of political exiles and the beginnings of the modern party system. Oil and dictatorship had centralised authority and created the foundations of a state which would distribute national resources among different social groups. The days of the regional *caudillos* were now long gone, and long repressed intellectual and business circles had a new, modernising vision of Venezuela.

A period of mass mobilisation led to the creation or expansion of AD, COPEI, the Communist Party and a myriad of trade unions, associations and peasant movements. The disappearance of Gómez's stifling authority encouraged a dramatic flowering of Venezuelan civil society. Yet despite these social changes, the next two unelected governments tried to suppress union activity and restrict party activity. In frustration, the AD leadership joined the military conspiracy which led to the *trienio* and Venezuela's first brief experience of democratic rule before the 1948 coup which brought yet another military ruler to power.

The last dictator

Like many Latin American dictators, General Marcos Pérez Jiménez had delusions of grandeur and an eye to posterity. Between 1948 and 1958 he presided over the reconstruction of Caracas, inaugurating luxury hotels, theatres and clubs for his loyal officers. His regime also built the first of the tower blocks which today fill the capital's skyline. His greatest folly was the Humboldt Hotel, perched on the top of Mount Avila and reached only by cable car.

Whether ruling directly or behind a civilian facade, Pérez Jiménez controlled Venezuela for ten years. He rolled back the reforms of the *trienio*, outlawed the political parties and repressed any form of opposition. As under Gómez, Venezuela's jails were again filled with union organisers and political activists. Torture was commonplace, and political assassinations terrorised the underground AD leadership.

Yet the economy seemed to boom as Pérez Jiménez increased oil production and extended leases to the foreign companies. As rural conditions worsened, hundreds of thousands of peasants flocked to Caracas and other cities. The capital's infamous shanty towns began to grow, even though the regime ordered them to be bulldozed.

Eventually, economic incompetence and corruption took its toll. The government refused to honour its debts to Venezuelan creditors and had no interest in cooperating with the country's more progressive business sectors. The Church, at first in favour of the regime, turned against it. A coup attempt failed, and Pérez Jiménez purged the military. When he lost the backing of the business elite, the Church, much of the military and the US, the dictator had no choice but to leave. Chastened by the experience of the *trienio*, AD and COPEI reemerged to sign the Pact of Punto Fijo and usher in the two-party system.

■ **The Great U-Turn**

Thirty years after Punto Fijo and six democratically elected governments later, Carlos Andrés Pérez was inaugurated as president for the second time on 16 February 1989. At a glittering champagne ceremony attended by 700 dignitaries and 24 heads of state, Pérez chose to speak out against Venezuela's debt burden. Little was said about the forthcoming policy shift.

The election campaign had taken place in an atmosphere of economic crisis. Servicing the country's US$33 billion debt was reported to be taking almost half the country's export earnings. Inflation was running at 35 per cent. Growth of 4.2 per cent was largely due to AD predecessor President Lusinchi's spending on public-sector programmes. The country's foreign reserves had been spent, and oil prices were stagnant. Yet Pérez had skirted round the issue of austerity and economic reform in his election campaign. The biggest issue had instead been a rumbling dispute with Colombia over control of coastal waters around Lake Maracaibo.

Eleven days after the inauguration Caracas was shaken by the *caracazo*, the worst disturbances the capital had seen since 1958. The immediate spark for the explosion was the rise in bus fares which had come into force over the weekend. This was the first effect of a range of economic measures which the government had announced after the inauguration ceremony. These included a single floating exchange rate for the *bolívar*, the removal of most price controls, a programme of public spending cuts and a rise in domestic fuel prices. The reforms, said the government, had been approved by the International Monetary Fund in return for a US$4.3 billion loan to assist with its balance of payments.

The so-called 'IMF riots' caused alarm in Caracas, Washington and elsewhere in Latin America and enabled Pérez to obtain further loans and to reschedule some of the existing debt. They also forced him to slow down his reform programme, albeit temporarily. Above all, they showed the extent of opposition to the free-market U-turn. As Pérez persisted in his reforms, this opposition took different and dramatic forms.

The military

Since the departure of Pérez Jiménez the Venezuelan military had been a mostly passive spectator of political events. After several abortive coup attempts by right-wing factions during Betancourt's presidency, the armed forces became more institutionalised and 'apolitical'. Oil wealth paid for equipment and above-average salaries, while the culture of corruption ensured that high-ranking officers remained loyal to the system. The minister of defence has always been a senior officer.

The military showed its loyalty to the system in the 1960s when it effectively contained a small-scale guerrilla campaign led by the PCV and other left-wing groups. In the event, the governments of Leoni and Caldera negotiated peace and the insurgents laid down their arms, but the military had shown its commitment to the two-party democracy. In the following years the armed forces were more concerned with what they saw as domestic subversion.

During the oil boom years the military budget expanded generously. Spending tripled in the early 1980s despite the fall in oil prices and top officers were implicated in a series of lucrative scandals involving the purchase of equipment and alleged drug smuggling.

But by the mid-1980s the economic crisis was taking its toll on the military. Young officers saw their salaries drop in value and lower ranking soldiers experienced real hardship. The allegations of corruption which surrounded the presidency of Jaime Lusinchi intensified when Pérez took office and infuriated large sectors of the military. Gradually a split emerged between some junior officers, committed to reform and clean government, and most of the higher echelons.

The February 1992 coup attempt: tanks in the streets of Caracas.

(Wesley Bocme/Rex Features)

A tale of two coups

The rumours started in November 1991 and intensified for two months. On 4 February 1992 five army units attacked the defence ministry, the Caracas military airport and other targets. Their main aim was to assassinate President Pérez, who first escaped from his residence and then the presidential palace. Pérez's life was saved by loyal troops who eventually put down the rebellion. The fighting was shortlived and fierce; 14 troops died, 50 were wounded and more than 1,000 rebels were arrested. As many as 80 civilians died in the crossfire.

The coup attempt created a national hero, Lt Col Hugo Chávez, leader of the so-called Revolutionary Bolivarian Movement, who appeared on television to call an end to the fighting. But while Pérez dismissed the coup as 'the last roar of militarism', Chávez promised that there would be 'other opportunities'.

The second coup attempt started on 27 November and lasted two days. This time rebel aircraft bombed the presidential palace amidst heavy fighting in Caracas and at the military base in Maracay. More than 170 people were killed and 1,000 soldiers arrested, while others escaped to Peru. Again, troops loyal to the government overcame the rebels.

In a bizarre twist, a video showing two uniformed senior officers calling for popular support was replaced at the last moment in the national TV studios by another which featured three gun-wielding guerrillas. The broadcast did little to help the rebels, and some analysts accused the government of conniving in the coup as a means of discrediting Chávez.

The left

The military interventions were symptoms of a wider rejection of Pérez and his policies. As the economic reforms produced growing hardship and allegations of corruption intensified, trade unions and political parties began to lead the opposition. Shortly after the second coup attempt, local and regional elections brought victories for COPEI as well as two parties of the left.

The first, the MAS, has been Venezuela's third party since 1971, when it was formed by former Communists and ex-guerrillas. Politically, it is situated between the PCV and AD's social democracy, with strong support in several states and an average vote of about ten per cent. Although it is strongly opposed to corruption, critics accuse it of sharing some of the worst features of AD-COPEI *partidocrácia*. More unexpected was Causa R's victory, in which an unknown schoolteacher, Aristóbulo Isturiz won the mayorship of Caracas against a senior AD politician. Other good results suggested that Causa R was breaking out of its Guayana stronghold and becoming a national force, a development reinforced by the December 1993 presidential election result.

Causa R, with its roots in the labour movement, bears some similarity to the Workers' Party in Brazil. After many years of involvement in the SIDOR plant in Ciudad Guayana, the party and its leader, Andrés Velásquez, enjoy massive support in Bolívar State. Rejecting the label of Marxism and describing itself as 'radically democratic', Causa R lacks a clearly defined programme but has a reputation for honesty and local accountability. It is liable to remain a serious force in Venezuelan politics.

Back to the Future

With Pérez gone and Caldera returned, political commentators predict a wholesale reversal of the economic reform programme over the next few years. Caldera's earliest moves certainly suggest a return to old-style Venezuelan government. Staple food prices were fixed by a 'voluntary price stabilisation' policy, petrol prices were untouched, Caldera promised a package of measures against waste and corruption. Most revealingly, the President immediately adopted an 'emergency' constitutional provision to rule by decree.

But Caldera's room for manoeuvre is. His *Convergencia* and MAS supporters in Congress have only a quarter of the seats. The big AD and COPEI blocs are hostile to the President's programme, while Causa R refuses to be drawn into an alliance. Conflict is inevitable, especially as the old parties control congressional committees.

Even more inevitable is continuing economic hardship. With low oil prices, dwindling foreign investment, continuing high inflation, a massive projected US$6 billion 1994 budget deficit and the economy in recession, further austerity measures cannot be far away.

3 ECONOMY

Boom and Bust

One day in December 1922 Venezuela's economic destiny changed for good. A Shell-owned oil exploration team was drilling on the eastern shore of Lake Maracaibo. The technicians knew that some oil was to be found there; a few wells were already producing an insignificant amount of crude. A small oil industry had been established in Venezuela since 1917, but its techniques were primitive and output disappointing.

As the team drilled the well it had named Los Barrosos 2, it suddenly struck a massive reserve of oil. Within hours an estimated 100,000 barrels of high-quality crude oil had blown out through the rig.

The first European explorers had noticed a strange black material in the lake and swampy shores of Maracaibo. The indigenous communities used the sticky fluid to caulk and repair their canoes and to trap animals. The Spaniards dismissed the 'devil's excrement' and left the inhospitable Maracaibo region on the margins of the colony.

The development of petroleum technology was to bring Venezuela, and Maracaibo in particular, a dramatic change in fortune. Today, Maracaibo is the country's second city, a modern, expensive high-rise metropolis, home to a cosmopolitan population of oil engineers and executives. Venezuela's oil fields now stretch across many parts of the country, including the vast Orinoco belt with its enormous untapped potential, but Maracaibo remains the oil capital, with its hundreds of derricks bristling from the lake.

■ Black Gold

At 13 us cents a litre, petrol in Venezuela costs much less than the bottled water that the middle classes drink with their Scotch. Not surprisingly, the seemingly endless supply of cheap petrol has spawned a motor car culture of impressive proportions. Venezuela boasts a network of modern, well maintained roads, and Caracas is criss-crossed by six-lane highways, permanently jammed with angry, hooting queues of us-built gas guzzlers. Venezuela also claims the world's worst record for deaths by road accident.

Venezuela currently produces about 2.5 million barrels of oil per day (bpd). Of that it exported almost 2.1 million bpd in 1993 at an average export price of us$15 per barrel. With proven reserves of 63 billion barrels, the largest outside the Middle East, the country could continue to export at the present rate for more than seventy years.

Oil and gas exports earned Venezuela just under us$11 billion in 1993, representing more than 80 per cent of total export earnings. The industry has traditionally provided the government with at least 40 per cent of its revenues. Since 1976, when the oil industry was nationalised, the Venezuelan state has controlled exploration, extraction and refining through the state holding company, Petróleos de Venezuela SA (PDVSA) and its various subsidiaries.

Venezuela is the third largest producer (after Saudi Arabia and Iran) within the Organisation of Petroleum Exporting Countries (OPEC), of which it is a founding member, and the ninth largest in the world. Its production currently accounts for about 3 per cent of the world's total. The country has ambitious plans to increase production to 3.1 million bpd by the end of the century.

As well as selling crude oil, Venezuela also exports refined petroleum and other oil products. Thanks to investment in refining and transportation, 31 per cent of the country's petroleum exports in 1993 were refined and 69 per cent crude. PDVSA has interests in North American and European companies and has storage facilities in Belgium, the Netherlands, Germany and the US.

But while oil has brought Venezuela intermittent bonanzas, it has also proved unpredictable. The boom years between 1973 and 1983 pulled in an estimated US$150 billion and created the myth of 'Saudi Venezuela'. But since the mid-1980s, prices have been unstable and often disastrously low. In 1981, for instance, a barrel fetched US$30 on the world market; by 1986, the price had dropped to US$12.

With its boom and bust history, Venezuela's oil industry has not brought economic stability. Nor has it provided employment for more than a tiny percentage of Venezuelans. Instead, it has posed the difficult question of how to distribute the wealth from a national resource within a highly unequal society.

■ The Colonial Economy

Before oil changed the face of Venezuela, the country was first an undeveloped colonial outpost and then an unstable exporter of agricultural commodities. European colonists first arrived looking for gold with little success, although they found pearls around the island of Cubagua and forced Indian slaves to dive for them. They also set up a salt extraction industry on the Araya peninsula near Cumaná. Gradually the colony expanded inland and ranches were established on the seemingly limitless *llanos*. Leather became an important export, together with cacao, wheat and tobacco.

Officially, Venezuela was locked into a monopolistic relationship with Spain and other parts of the Spanish empire. In reality, however, Venezuelan entrepreneurs were involved in considerable contraband trade in cacao and tobacco with Dutch, English and French merchants who came and went freely from the poorly defended Caribbean coast.

The country's various regions had distinct economic activities and markets. There was some internal trade in cattle and crops, linking the Andes, the coastal region and the *llanos.* But each of these areas also looked outwards independently. The western Andean region had links with Colombia and the important centre of Bogotá; the coastal districts traded with islands such as Cuba, Puerto Rico and Santo Domingo. Only in the mid-18th century did Caracas establish itself as the undisputed centre and capital of Venezuela.

Chocolate Money

It was the cacao boom which began in the mid-17th century which helped push Caracas to economic preeminence. The indigenous cacao plant thrived in the warm coastal valleys, and Venezuelan cacao enjoyed an unparalleled reputation. The early trade was mostly with Mexico, where the unusually sweet Venezuelan crop had a protected market and fetched good prices. Dutch traders were willing to pay even better prices, as they established their reputation for making superior chocolate.

The cacao boom reinforced the wealth and power of a tiny landowning oligarchy. This elite, known popularly as the *gran cacao,* imported luxury consumer goods from Europe, and enjoyed a whirl of lavish social and cultural events in Caracas and Cumaná. At the same time, the black slaves whose work ensured the prosperity of the *gran cacao,* lived in poverty.

Coffee

The independence wars and the instability which followed ended Venezuela's cacao boom and ushered in a new export commodity. With much of the country in ruins, the cacao plantations were neglected or destroyed and their slaves dispersed. The link with Spain was now broken, and Venezuela had to find its place in a new trading relationship with North America and Europe.

Tastes were changing in Europe, where coffee was replacing cocoa as the favourite beverage, and European exporters happily provided high-interest loans to landowners who wished to produce coffee. As a result, the 1830s witnessed another boom in which coffee plantations spread rapidly.

Like cacao, coffee production was exclusively export-oriented. But whereas the colonial cacao trade at least carried the guarantee of relatively stable prices, coffee was traded on the unregulated world market. When the coffee boom faltered and then collapsed in the late 1840s, it left the Venezuelan economy bankrupt and over-dependent on a single commodity. Nevertheless, coffee brought some prosperity to Venezuela's small and medium-sized landowners and provided work for poor landless peasants and agricultural labourers from Colombia.

■ The Petrol Phenomenon

The Venezuelan economy at the beginning of the 20th century was backward and internationally insignificant. Although it had become the world's second largest coffee exporter after Brazil, the country had little other income and almost no industry. Its cities were small and the vast majority of people lived in rural poverty. Only an estimated 1,000 big landowners did well from coffee, which accounted for 80 per cent of exports. Yet even they were hard hit when the price for a 100 kg bag of coffee fell from 5.47 *bolívares* in 1895 to 0.83 *bolívares* in 1898.

Within forty years the discovery of oil catapulted Venezuela from impoverished obscurity into spectacular wealth, transforming it from one of Latin America's poorest countries to by far its richest. Petroleum changed Venezuela into an urban society, gave it a North American consumer culture and broke the power of the traditional landowning elites. It also introduced new and complex relationships between Venezuelan governments and foreign oil companies.

The 1922 Maracaibo oil find triggered a massive expansion in Venezuelan exports. In 1920-21 the country exported 100,000 barrels, worth less than one ninth of coffee exports in the same period. By 1926-7 the figure was over six million barrels, and in 1935-6 nearly 23 million barrels, worth twenty times more than coffee earnings. From the mid-1920s until the Second World War, Venezuela was the world's second largest oil producer (after the US) and its biggest exporter.

The oil rush attracted petrol companies from North America and Europe, which were warmly welcomed by the dictator Gómez. Running the country as his personal fiefdom, Gómez initially gave or sold large tracts of land to his supporters and cronies who sold drilling concessions to the companies. As the industry expanded, however, Gómez sought to redefine this relationship. A law in 1922, reputedly drafted by representatives of the oil firms, regulated royalty payments as a percentage of refined petroleum's price on the world market but also granted long leases and generous tax breaks.

Profit and Loss

The system established by Gómez lasted until 1943. It brought the oil companies incredible profits as Shell, Standard Oil and Gulf controlled 99 per cent of production by the end of the 1930s. In contrast, the Venezuelan state received between 10 and 20 per cent of profits. But even this was an unprecedented windfall for Gómez and his clique.

The losers were those who worked in the oil industry. Although marginally better than those in agriculture, conditions were appalling for badly paid Venezuelans who lived in primitive camps. Contemporary accounts describe shanty towns built around the hot and disease-ridden Lake Maracaibo, with several workers sharing a single windowless hovel.

The old and the new: the lake
Maracaibo oilfield.
(Julio Etchart/Reportage)

A worker's monthly wage in 1936 was 42 *bolívares;* food, rent and
transport, however, amounted to 43.5 *bolívares.* Foreign workers, on the
other hand, particularly North Americans, earned at least double this wage.

'Sowing the Oil'

With the death of Gómez in 1935 and the gradual transition towards
democracy in Venezuela, the question of ownership and control of
Venezuelan oil became a political controversy. The reformist, nationalist
activists of AD believed that the state should get a better deal from the oil
companies and increase Venezuelan involvement in the industry. In the
phrase of Arturo Uslar Pietri, the nationalists wanted the state to 'sow the
oil' and invest its wealth in long-term development. Labour disputes and
growing working-class mobilisation were also exerting pressure on the
companies.

After disputes with the companies, the government of Isaías Medina
Angarita negotiated a new agreement in 1943 which raised royalties and
taxes, especially on profits. In return, the companies obtained extensions on
their concessions of up to 40 years. The agreement took place against the
background of the Second World War and increasing US demand for oil.
The companies also feared that Venezuela might follow the example of
Mexico, which had nationalised its oil industry in 1938.

Nationalisation and OPEC

Hostilities between the Venezuelan state and the oil companies ceased in
1976 when Carlos Andrés Pérez nationalised the oil, gas and coal
industries. This followed disagreements over royalty payments, taxes and
pricing, whether Venezuela should be allowed to construct its own refineries

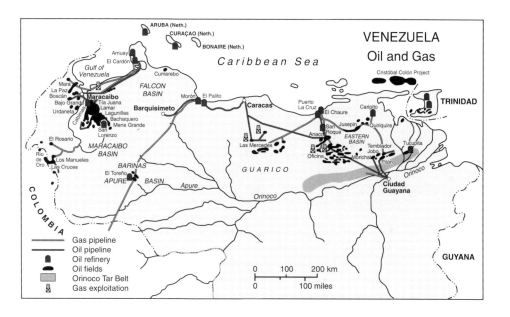

Orimulsion: A Sticky Future

Alongside its reserves of 63 billion barrels, Venezuela also claims a further 270 billion barrels of extra heavy crude oil in the so-called Orinoco Tar Belt. The problem with this oil is its density; the crude looks like a sticky brown treacle and has to undergo a costly upgrading and refining process before it can be sold as petroleum.

In the mid-1980s PDVSA collaborated with British Petroleum in a venture to sidestep the problem. The result was Orimulsion, a mixture of bitumen, water and a secret stabiliser, which can be used to fire power stations and other generators.

Unfortunately for PDVSA, Orimulsion soon earned a reputation as 'the world's dirtiest fuel' and ran into trouble with environmental agencies over alleged emissions of sulphur dioxide and nitrogen oxide. Although PDVSA denies that Orimulsion is dirtier than coal, potential buyers have been discouraged. Projections that PDVSA would export 40 million tons annually by 1996 have proved unrealistic; current sales are only 5 million tonnes, of which the British company, Powergen, imports 1.3 million tons. Significantly, BP sold its stake in the Orimulsion marketing company in late 1993.

Venezuela is now in search of foreign investment to make fuller use of the Orinoco Tar Belt. The worry among government and PDVSA executives is that the country could be left with huge reserves of 'dirty', unsellable crude in an increasingly environmentally conscious world.

and whether technology and skills were being transferred from companies to the state. Most important was the question of sovereignty and control over the country's natural resources and whether Venezuela should progress from being a 'landlord state' to a fully-fledged producer, refiner and exporter.

The Venezuelan government had already shown its determination to take on the multinationals in 1960, when it played a key role in the founding of the Organisation of Petroleum Exporting Countries (OPEC). Conscious of the threat posed to its exports to the US by plentiful and cheap oil in the Middle East, it argued that exporters such as Saudi Arabia and Iran would reap better prices from the bargaining position of a cartel.

The creation of OPEC had two consequences for Venezuelan oil. Its member states set agreed production quotas, thus preventing over-production and a destructive price war between producer countries. With OPEC's new pricing policy producers set the price for their oil rather than receiving a percentage of the world market price set by the companies.

OPEC was able to take maximum advantage of the crisis caused by the 1973 Arab-Israeli War and the Arab embargo against the West, when the price of a barrel jumped from US$1.76 in 1970 to US$10.31 in 1974. In 1974 alone, Venezuelan income rose by 40 per cent and government revenues by 170 per cent.

With the sudden influx of petrodollars, the time seemed right for nationalisation. Buoyed up by OPEC's success, the Pérez government took two years to complete the takeover, avoiding serious conflict with the companies, even though their agreed US$1 billion in compensation was only partly paid. Their concessions, negotiated in 1943, were in any case due to expire in 1983 and they were more interested in the cheaper and higher-grade oil to be found in the Middle East.

The creation of PDVSA as a semi-autonomous company brought problems, as it struggled for political independence while the government tried to extract maximum tax revenue. In the following years the government made PDVSA sell petrol on the domestic market at under cost price, hand over its foreign earnings to the Central Bank and pay huge taxes. Even so, with the impetus provided by the oil boom between 1973 and 1983, PDVSA established itself as an important force in the world oil industry.

The End of the Party

On the eve of nationalisation, a US academic wrote optimistically that 'Venezuela stands on the threshold of what seems, thanks to oil, an unbelievably bright and prosperous future.' Little more than two decades later, much of that brightness has worn off as Venezuela heads into *la noche postpetrolera* ('the post-petroleum night').

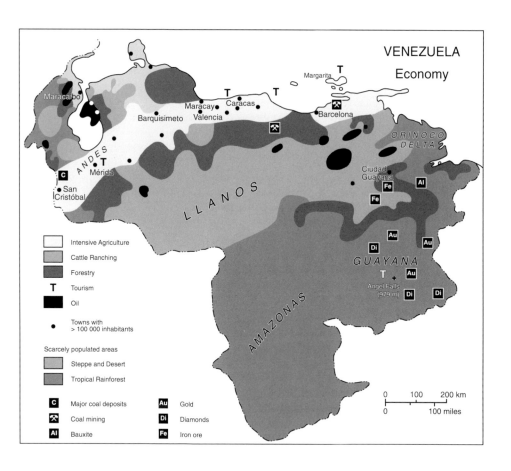

Several factors contributed to Venezuela's fall from economic grace and its current problems. After the 1973 oil shock, western countries were determined to avoid further dramatic price rises by diversifying energy sources in areas such as the North Sea and Alaska. They also tried to cut demand through increased power efficiency and conservation measures. As a result, OPEC's share of world production shrank from 70 per cent in the early 1970s to 50 per cent a decade later. Venezuela's world share, meanwhile, fell from 10.4 per cent in 1967 to a mere 5 per cent in 1984.

Since 1973 there have been other, albeit brief, upturns. The Iranian revolution and Iraq-Iran War produced a boom between 1978 and 1981 when the barrel price rose from US$13 to US$34, but by 1986 the price was again under US$13. In 1990 the Gulf War produced another windfall, with the price briefly touching US$40, but by 1992 the price had dropped back to US$16.7. The general prospects for oil prices in the 1990s are uninspiring.

The Debt Trap

The golden years brought other unfortunate consequences. Thanks to the revenues of the early 1970s, the Pérez government encouraged massive imports of goods, both for everyday and luxury consumption as well as for developing national industries. Billions of the dollars brought in by oil immediately left the country again, bound for private bank accounts in New York and Geneva. Because the *bolívar* was artificially overvalued and interest rates low, speculators could buy dollars cheaply and invest them abroad in high-interest accounts.

Worse, despite the huge influx of oil dollars, Pérez and his successors borrowed freely from the international banks in order to fund their ambitious spending programmes. Following Pérez, the government of Luís Herrera Campins increased spending still further. By 1984, the country's debt stood at US$34 billion. As many of the loans were short-term and high-interest, the fall in oil prices was disastrous. In 1982, for instance, it was estimated that debt service payments due that year would take up nearly 95 per cent of oil revenues.

Determined at first to maintain debt payments and continue high levels of public spending, Herrera Campins simply spent Venezuela's international reserves and printed more money. Politicians and ordinary Venezuelans alike seemingly did not want to acknowledge that the oil boom was over.

The decision by Herrera Campins to devalue the *bolívar* on 'Black Friday', 28 February 1983 was inevitable. Introducing a complex three-tier exchange mechanism, the government let the national currency float against the dollar. Within a year, the *bolívar*'s value had fallen three-fold. Unemployment and inflation soared; investment and GDP plummeted. Between 1981 and 1989 Venezuela's GDP declined by almost 4 per cent and per capita income by one-quarter.

■ The Quest for Diversification

Agriculture: Fallow Fields

Little of Venezuela's huge landscape is cultivated. The strip of land which joins Caracas, Maracay, Valencia and Barquisimeto has plenty of well-managed farms, where cocoa, coffee, citrus and sugar flourish in the tropical climate and fertile soil. Further inland, however, farms become more isolated, villages more remote and fields of crops give way to scrubland, forest or the flat pasture of the *llanos*.

Only 11 per cent of the Venezuelan labour force now works in agriculture (down from 45 per cent in the 1960s), and the sector contributes less than 6 per cent of GDP. One-fifth of the country's land is devoted to farming, and of that pasture for cattle-raising accounts for 75 per cent.

Agriculture's decline largely stems from oil. Particularly in the boom years, oil provoked a drift to the cities and wholescale abandonment of villages and smallholdings. Oil revenues paid for imports and subsidised urban food prices, undercutting demand for locally produced goods.

Another obstacle to Venezuelan agriculture is the failure of governments to bring about effective land reform. Since the end of the Gómez dictatorship, each government has promised to increase access to land and services for the country's peasantry. But figures from the 1988 agricultural census show that holdings of under 20 hectares made up 73 per cent of all farms but covered a mere 4 per cent of total arable land. Farms of more than 500 hectares, on the other hand, represented 3 per cent of holdings but covered 70 per cent of land.

Cattle-raising is the most obvious agricultural activity, and in large parts of the country cattle roam seemingly unhindered across enormous ranches. The 13.5 million cattle recorded in 1991 are responsible for Venezuela's self-sufficiency in milk and mostly go to satisfy a national craving for giant-sized steaks.

Venezuela imports between 20 and 40 per cent of its food each year, mostly as wheat from the US and beans from other South American countries. Foreign multinationals such as Kraft and Nestlé and their local subsidiaries dominate the domestic food processing market. The main export crop is coffee, reputedly one of the best varieties in the world. In 1992 Venezuela's farmers produced one million 60 kg bags of coffee (compared to Colombia's 15 million bags), but exported less than 20 per cent, earning US$11 million.

Other Natural Resources

Oil is not Venezuela's only natural resource. In the wilderness of Guayana lie huge deposits of iron ore, bauxite, gold, silver, uranium, nickel and phosphates. In the purpose-built modern metropolis of Ciudad Guayana, steel mills, aluminium processing plants and concrete factories belch out smoke and dust which cover the surrounding vegetation in a fine white powder. A hundred miles south of Ciudad Guayana lies the Guri dam which generates more than 10,000 MW of hydroelectricity from the Caroní river. The electricity powers the industrial activity of the new city downstream, but also reaches Caracas.

Since the discovery of oil, Venezuelan governments have recognised the dangers of over-reliance on a single commodity. In an attempt to 'sow the oil', the first Pérez administration invested heavily in such 'strategic industries' as steel, bauxite and aluminium during the 1970s, nationalising US facilities and aiming at increased output.

A series of public-sector companies come together under the umbrella of the Corporación Venezolana de Guayana (CVG), which is a loss-making state-owned holding company and the eighth largest business in Latin

America. CVG controls more or less every aspect of life in the Guayana region, owning subsidiaries in mining, smelting, electricity and manufacturing. These companies operate on a grand scale; the Interalúmina bauxite processing plant, for instance, recorded output of 850,000 tonnes in 1990, while Siderúrgico de Orinoco (SIDOR), the steel company, produced 20.4 million tonnes of steel the same year.

Impressive as these figures are, CVG is in serious financial trouble. In 1992 the company's aluminium sector lost some 20 billion *bolívares* (US$330 million), and SIDOR and the electricity subsidiaries also reported heavy losses. Alcasa, the aluminium producing subsidiary, had production costs that year of US$1,400 per tonne yet was receiving only US$1,000 per tonne on the world market. The company has blamed the international recession and falling export demand for the poor results, although critics allege that it is inefficient and corrupt.

The Private Sector: Family Business

Because oil dominates Venezuela and oil is dominated by the state (and before that by foreign companies), the country's private sector is relatively young, weak and unimportant. Most private companies were founded in the 1960s and 1970s when the government encouraged the building of domestic industries to reduce dependence on imported goods. Many private companies tend to be small or medium-sized and mostly produce manufactured goods for the domestic and regional markets. Commerce, services and construction are considered more lucrative than industry, and it is often recent immigrants to Venezuela who have started industrial concerns.

There is a significant automobile industry in Venezuela with large private-sector investment, but most non-state companies produce consumer goods such as food, building materials and textiles. A growing area of private-sector activity is the world of media and entertainment, in which television stations, soap operas and *salsa* CDs are lucrative business.

The private sector also has some large and powerful conglomerates. According to the social scientist, Daniel Hellinger: 'Of Venezuela's forty-five largest private, nationally-owned enterprises, thirty-nine [in the 1980s] were owned by a small coterie of families and economic groups; only six were listed on the public stock exchange. Most private firms had never undergone a transition of control and were closely held by about thirty-five major families and groups. These groups fiercely rival one another over some matters, but they suppress competition by keeping business within the family whenever possible.'

Names such as Cisneros (media, fast food and the Pepsi Cola franchise), Mendoza (automobile assembly) and Phelps (foodstuffs, radio, newspapers and airlines) are among the best known of the family business empires.

The Informal Sector

In Venezuela old cars never die, but are endlessly patched up, repaired and resprayed. Every small town has streets of garages and workshops, most no bigger than a garden shed, where mechanics labour to revive ancient petrol-thirsty vehicles. Retread tyres are sold on every street corner, and spare parts are piled high in tiny roadside shacks. In the hillside *barrios* of Caracas, a bewildering choice of workshops faces the poorer *Caraqueño* with a broken television or video. Among the maze of steep slum streets are countless small stores, bars and repair shops.

These are the most visible signs of the informal economy which employs an estimated 40 per cent of Venezuelans. The informal sector is difficult to define, but includes individuals and businesses which operate outside the 'measured' economy of central banks and international agencies. Informal businesses pay no taxes, do not observe labour laws and are usually small-scale. On the other hand, they offer valuable employment and often interlink with the formal economy in many ways.

But more and more Venezuelan workers are joining another branch of the informal sector, as companies, both state-sector and private, employ them on short-term contracts. This means that they are paid on a strictly hourly or piece-work rate, receive few or no benefits such as paid holidays, subsidised meals or health care, and have no union rights. Even state companies such as SIDOR are increasingly using contract labour, and more than half of the workforce in Ciudad Guayana is now employed under these conditions.

Privatisation

'Investors with a vision can see potential in Venezuela with its strategic geographic location in the north of South America, abundant natural resources, low labor costs, a sound economic reform program with ample incentives to foreign investment.' So claim the advertisements in North American and European newspapers from the Fondo de Inversiones de Venezuela (FIV), the agency in charge of privatising the country's economy.

As elsewhere in Latin America, state ownership, import substitution and economic protectionism have fallen into disrepute. Faced with huge budget deficits, a US$34 billion debt and loss-making state companies, the second Pérez administration embraced the gospel of privatisation as part of its economic reform plan. This stood in contrast to the state-oriented economic policy of the previous Pérez government which nationalised the oil industry and other sectors.

Privatisation, along with other radical economic restructuring, lay at the heart of Pérez's *gran viraje* ('great U-turn'). From 1989 onwards, the model of building up local industry to supply the local market was officially declared obsolete, to be replaced with an economic structure geared towards foreign investment and exports. Free trade replaced protectionism, privatisation superseded nationalisation.

In December 1991 a consortium headed by the US giant GTE bought a majority share of CANTV, the national telecommunications company. The sale brought the Venezuelan treasury nearly US$2 billion. Earlier that year the Spanish airline Iberia bought a 60 per cent stake in the Venezuelan state airline, VIASA, for US$145 million.

Since 1991, however the privatisation programme has slowed down, and there are doubts as to whether the policy will be pursued. Other possible targets for privatisation are three electrical companies, the domestic airline Aeropostal, and the loss-making Alcasa and other CVG subsidiaries. For the less ambitious investor, the 50,000-seater Caracas racecourse, La Rinconada, is also up for sale.

Supporters of privatisation claim that CANTV is proof of its success. In 1992 the company made a profit of US$169 million (compared to a loss of US$72 million the previous year), improved services dramatically and oversaw record levels of investment. Opponents warn, however, that the privatisation of 'strategic industries' such as aluminium and even oil will erode Venezuelan economic power and sovereignty.

Foreign Investment

The search for foreign capital is nothing new in Venezuela. During the period of industrialisation and import substitution funded by oil revenues, foreign companies, primarily from the US, invested heavily. Because many of the manufacturing plants were capital-intensive, Venezuela came to depend on foreign investment as well as transnational technology and management. If Venezuelan governments erected tariffs and handed out subsidies to protect domestic industry from foreign competition, they also welcomed financing from overseas.

Since 1989, companies from Italy, Spain, Japan and the US have made considerable investments in the petrochemical sector, while transnationals such as Nestlé, Heinz, BAT and Procter & Gamble have increased their stakes in food processing, tobacco and other consumer goods.

The most controversial area for foreign investment is the oil industry, the traditional symbol of Venezuelan economic nationalism and pride. In late 1993 PDVSA unveiled its US$45.8 billion investment plan for the next decade, stressing massively increased production. The company stated that it would itself invest US$29 billion and was looking for the remaining US$19.5 billion from foreign investors. The areas assigned to foreign companies are the so-called 'marginal fields', where there are relatively small volumes of production. PDVSA hopes that companies such as Shell, Exxon and Total will produce crude oil and sell it to the state.

In the 'Cristóbal Colón' project, PDVSA plans to work in partnership with

Shell, Exxon and Mitsubishi to produce natural gas from Caribbean offshore fields, transport it by pipeline to the Paria Peninisula and export liquefied gas to Europe and the US.

Foreign Trade

Since the advent of oil, Venezuela's main trading partner has been the US. Venezuela has traditionally exported crude oil and refined products and in return has imported machinery, chemicals and vehicles. In 1992, the US accounted for approximately half of all exports and imports.

But Venezuelan governments have been eager to diversify markets, and the country has played a leading role in regional trade blocs and agreements. The most important is the free trade agreement between Venezuela, Colombia and Ecuador, which has reduced barriers and established a common external tariff. As a result of the pact, signed in 1992, bilateral trade between Venezuela and Colombia increased by more than 200 per cent by the end of 1993 and trade with Ecuador by 60 per cent.

In another agreement signed with Chile in April 1993, most import tariffs are set to disappear by 1999, enabling the Venezuelan motor industry to explore new markets. A further free-trade pact signed with Mexico and Colombia (the so-called Group of Three) in December 1993 envisages a ten-year tariff reduction process, excluding agriculture and automobiles.

Venezuela has also signed an innovative one-way trade agreement with English-speaking Caribbean countries, allowing them to export goods duty-free into the Venezuelan market for a period of ten years. After that period, the agreement will become recriprocal, giving Venezuela free access to the Caribbean market. Under the San José Agreement, signed with Mexico in 1980, Venezuela further boosted its trading stature in the Caribbean and Central America by agreeing to supply petroleum on concessionary terms to ten countries. This arrangement is supposed to contribute to regional stability, but it also furthers Venezuela's economic and political ambitions in the Caribbean region.

Venezuela has tried to diversify its production and its markets. Some changes have undoubtedly taken place, and increased trade with Andean and Caribbean neighbours is helping the balance of payments. But oil still dominates the Venezuelan economy, and is likely to make up more than 80 per cent of export earnings for the foreseeable future.

4   SOCIETY

Plenty and Poverty

On the second and fourth Friday nights of each month the upmarket Caracas area of Altamira goes wild. The smart restaurants and bars are full to bursting point and even more cacophonous than usual with the hubbub of conversation, mobile phones and US rock music. Outside, boys watch over the massed ranks of BMWs and Land Cruisers in return for a small tip. The noise goes on into the small hours, when finally police cars with wailing sirens and loudhailers try to clear the streets of revellers. This is pay day in wealthy Caracas and a reminder that Venezuela still has a middle class which likes to spend its money.

Weekends in poor Caracas are also eventful. On Monday mornings, the newspapers carry a grim roll call of those killed in stabbings and shootings in the capital's *barrios*. The figure often reaches forty or fifty, mostly young, male and poor.

■ Two Venezuelas

The inhabitants of Caracas have an everyday vocabulary to distinguish between rich and poor. The hillsides inhabited by the wealthy are known as *lomas;* these desirable *urbanizaciones* or neighbourhoods, complete with lawns, exotic gardens and satellite dishes, are made up of large houses or *quintas.* Across town, the steep, denuded slopes where the poor live are called *cerros.* Here, their shacks or *ranchos* cling precariously to the hillside, with rough tracks or stairways leading between them. From a distance at night the poor districts or *barrios* look almost picturesque as their lights twinkle on the hills; close up, the bare light bulbs shine harshly through windows without glass.

The two cities, rich and poor, high rise and slum, meet in the Caracas Metro. This high-tech miracle of French engineering was opened in 1983 and runs a fast, reliable service from Catia in the west to Petare in the east, two of the city's most notorious *barrios.* In the spotless new trains, ragged children pass among the smartly dressed commuters handing out cards which read *Ayudame para comer* ('please help me to eat').

Rural to urban

Venezuela is now an overwhelmingly urban society, with 91 per cent of its 20 million people living in towns and cities and four million of them in Caracas itself. The urban explosion took place between 1940 and 1960, when the capital was transformed from a sleepy colonial city of about half a million people into today's modern metropolis.

Oil fuelled the growth of Caracas and other cities, not because people moved in order to work in the industry, but because oil money paid for a huge expansion in construction. Government spending on urban projects boomed during the 1940s and 1950s, especially during the Pérez Jiménez dictatorship. In order to house the incoming rural migrants, the government built new working-class housing complexes. The most infamous of these is the vast *23 de enero* block in western Caracas, named after the date of the dictator's flight and a grim testimony to his modernisation programme.

But if most Venezuelans choose to live in cities, it is because there is less work and fewer opportunities in the countryside. Despite the country's great beauty and agricultural potential, most rural areas are sparsely inhabited and under-resourced. The unequal concentration of land owner-ship has forced many peasants to leave the countryside. The official minimum salary is 25 per cent lower in rural districts than urban ones, yet food and other basics are not necessarily any cheaper. Schools, hospitals and housing are inferior, and entertainment is in short supply. Not surprisingly, it is the young who are especially drawn to the bright lights of the city.

Decline and fall

The halcyon days of 'Saudi Venezuela' are long gone. In the boom years of the 1970s Venezuelans were disparaged by other Latin Americans for what seemed to be an undeserved windfall. The myth of the free-spending, tasteless *nouveau riche* took hold, and Venezuela became known as the highest per capita importer of Scotch whisky in the world. The motto of the typical Venezuelan shopper in Miami – *está barato, dame dos* ('it's cheap, I'll take two') seemed to symbolise a country with more money than sense.

The oil boom did pay for social improvements. The first Pérez government invested in public health and education. Thousands of young Venezuelans were able to study overseas through state scholarships, expanding the country's technocracy and swelling the ranks of the middle class. The boom also kept the social peace by enabling government to subsidise basic foods and medicines, fund a range of social programmes and contain political unrest.

The middle class did well out of the state spending spree. It has been estimated, for example, that only 40 per cent of subsidised goods were consumed by the poor and that the rest went to middle-income consumers or were even exported by 'creative entrepreneurs'. With party patronage and corruption rife, the social programmes were largely a failure. Despite spending up to 40 per cent of the state budget on social welfare (the highest per capita social expenditure in Latin America), Venezuela had worse poverty indicators in the 1970s than other poorer neighbours.

The real beneficiaries of the oil wealth were those who were already rich. In 1980 the national census estimated that 43 per cent of households were living in poverty. Venezuela had Latin America's highest average per capita income, but it was clear that the oil money was not trickling down to many.

Shrinking incomes

Since 1981 the ranks of Venezuela's poor have grown hugely, especially in the wake of President Pérez's economic reforms. According to the central statistical office, those defined as poor rose by 120 per cent in a decade, reaching almost eight million in 1990. In its 1991 report, the human rights organisation PROVEA claimed that 80 per cent of Venezuelans lived in poverty, a figure dismissed by President Pérez as 'irresponsible'.

However poverty is defined, it is clear that the national minimum wage (set at 9,000 *bolívares* per month for urban workers and 7,000 for rural workers in 1992) does not even cover the 11,200 *bolívares* estimated by the Central Bank to be the cost of an average family's monthly food bill. The *bolívar*'s devaluation has meant that the urban minimum wage's dollar value fell from US$120 in February 1992 to US$91 in September 1993. Pérez's gradual abolition of subsidies and the introduction of Value Added Tax (VAT) further pushed up consumer prices. In March 1994, the new Caldera administration promised to raise the private-sector minimum wage to 12,500 *bolívares*.

Yet with inflation running at 46 per cent in 1993, incomes have been seriously eroded. A minimum wage now buys around one-third of what it bought in 1984. Perhaps the worst affected are those living on pensions and the estimated 41 per cent of workers who do not even receive the statutory minimum.

■ Social Crisis
Health

Health indicators and services have declined alongside incomes since the reform programme took effect. Reduced budgets and privatisation of medical services have reduced poor Venezuelans' access to treatment. The health budget was halved between 1980 and 1990, and machinery and hospital buildings are not being properly maintained or modernised.

Venezuela's health statistics are not impressive. PROVEA estimates that one in five Venezuelan children suffers from malnutrition. The infant mortality rate stands at 35 per 1,000 live births, three times higher than Cuba and 80 per cent higher than Chile. Previously contained diseases such as malaria are making a comeback. Medicines are no longer available free of charge, and prices rose by almost 2,000 per cent between 1982 and 1992.

CARACAS

Mural of Simón Bolívar and the flags of the countries he has liberated. The design of the Venezuelan flag dates back to 1811. Yellow and red are the colours of Spain which are separated by blue as a symbol of the sea. Since 1817 there have been seven white stars in the blue band, symbolizing the seven provinces which made up the 1811 Venezuelan Confederation.
(Source: Flags Documentation Centre of the Netherlands)

The capital's spectacular mountain setting.
(Edward Paine/Last Frontiers)

Office blocks and shanty towns meet.
(Ricardo Bravo)

Caracas lies in a valley, its high-rise glass and concrete architecture ringed by what were once lushly forested mountains. Now many of the surrounding hillsides are covered with red brick, plywood and corrugated iron – the building materials of the city's shanty towns. Even from the gleaming futuristic Parque Central complex which houses theatres, galleries and expensive shops, it is impossible to ignore the hundreds of thousands of shacks which encircle the city. Little remains of the capital's once beautiful colonial centre, which was largely replaced with multi-storey office and apartment blocks. With the influx of immigrants from Europe in the 1940s and 1950s alongside rural incomers, the capital's authorities could not keep pace with demand for housing, and shanty towns mushroomed. The slums were already well established by the 1960s and have

Shoe shining in the Plaza Bolívar.
(John Thirtle/Geodyssey)

A working-class district.
(Ricardo Bravo)5

A recent shanty town settlement, La Vega *barrio*.
(Alan Gilbert)

continued to spread east and west out of the city centre. Some early slums have become established working-class areas over the years. The arrival of electricity, drinking water and roads gradually turned shanty towns into suburbs, while individual families slowly transformed their *ranchos* into solid homes. Other shanty towns, especially the most recent, are still without basic services and are breeding grounds for crime and disease.

An older slum district in central Caracas.
(Alan Gilbert)

A city dominated by cars: a Caracas freeway.
(Paddy Donnelly)

A piece of old Caracas: the
Plaza Bolívar.
(Sandy Markwick)
Bevrijder' op de achtergrond.
(Foto: Sandy Markwick)

Las Mercedes shopping centre:
an oasis of consumerism.
(Ricardo Bravo)

Baseball: the national passion.
(Ricardo Bravo)

zoals hier in een volkswijk.
(Foto: Ricardo Bravo)

Inside a shanty town home,
Caracas.
(Amnesty International)

Education

Education was one of the successes brought about by the oil windfall years. Between 1970 and 1980 governments invested heavily in education, creating a number of technical institutes and opening up university education to a wide social range. The aim of universal access to education was almost achieved and Venezuela began to match 'First World' standards.

Since the 1980s, however, education has also fallen victim to economic reform and austerity. Budget cuts reduced textbook provision by no less than 96 per cent between 1978 and 1989. As an average teacher's monthly salary is 14,000 *bolívares* (US$130), many are forced to do other jobs to make ends meet. While the private sector is expanding rapidly (accounting for nearly 17 per cent of school places in 1992), the public sector received a cut of more than US$10 million that year. Drop-out rates are alarmingly high, claims PROVEA, estimating that 1.2 million Venezuelans between 14 and 24 are neither in education nor work.

Housing

Of all Venezuela's social ills, housing is perhaps the most visible. Urban squalor is not just a problem in Caracas. Large cities such as Valencia and Barquisimeto also have their surrounding *barrios,* and even the picturesque Andean resort of Mérida has slum quarters. In the new city of Ciudad Guayana, the modern administrative quarter of Puerto Ordaz, with its high rise offices and shopping malls, contrasts with the sprawling slums of San Félix, the working-class district just across the river Caroní.

Between 40 and 60 per cent of people live in 'marginal' settlements in Caracas, Maracaibo and Ciudad Guayana, according to the national census office. The private-sector Chamber of Construction claims that 100,000 new homes would have to be built every year to keep pace with demand. In 1993, fewer than 9,000 were actually constructed.

The housing crisis has many dimensions. Land tenure in urban areas is often precarious, and squatters can be evicted to make way for residential or industrial development. High interest rates have made mortgages a near impossibility for lower-income families. At the same time, budget cuts have all but stopped government investment in public-sector housing and have led to serious degeneration of existing housing stock. Water provision, sewerage and electricity supply are all under increasing strain.

The poor must therefore build their own homes, despite inflationary increases in the price of materials such as cement and zinc roofing. As the best land around the cities is already taken, they must move ever further out to areas largely devoid of services or amenities. The combination of rudimentary building materials and unsuitable terrain can sometimes prove fatal when heavy rain creates devastating landslides in the hillside *barrios.*

The environment

A seemingly permanent layer of smog hangs over Caracas, trapped in the valley which shelters the capital city. Looking down from the shanty town hillside of Catia, the tower blocks and motorways of the modern metropolis shimmer in a carbon monoxide haze. As several large factories such as the notorious La Vega cement plant pump toxic fumes into the atmosphere, Caracas is becoming badly polluted. The authorities tried to cut down on car pollution in the 1980s by introducing the so-called *día de parada* (no driving day), when cars were banned from the roads on a rota according to their number plates. Rich *Caraqueños* merely bought another car to get round the ban, pushing the per capita vehicle ownership figure to one of the world's highest.

It is not just Caracas which is polluted. Many nearby beaches, especially those close to the port of La Guaira, are clogged with oil, litter and sewage. Oil has also seriously damaged Lake Maracaibo, where leaking underwater pipes have reportedly made the water unsafe for swimming. Environmental

Corruption

One of Caracas' more unlikely bestsellers is the three-volume *Dictionary of Corruption*. This 1,000-page tome meticulously details endless cases of financial impropriety and scandal among Venezuela's business and political elite. Corruption has become a way of life in Venezuelan politics, to the point where the established parties are largely discredited among most voters. Because of the country's oil wealth, large state sector and traditions of patronage, corruption reaches all levels of society. But few cases are as flagrant as those of the former president himself, Carlos Andrés Pérez.

When Pérez was reelected in 1988, he had already been censured by Congress for financial irregularities during his previous presidency. This time, he promised to stamp out corruption. But in May 1993 the president was indicted by the Supreme Court and suspended from office, accused of misappropriating 250 million *bolívares* from secret government funds. Pérez allegedly had the money converted at a special rate of 14.5 to the dollar a few days before the *bolívar* slumped to 34 with the removal in 1989 of the multiple exchange rate system.

Some critics of Pérez accuse him of pocketing the money directly; others claim that he used it to fund secret political activities. The most damning evidence was photocopied transaction statements from banks in New York, Paris, Geneva, Buenos Aires, Hong Kong and the Philippines. The accounts had been opened by Pérez himself and his mistress, Cecilia Matos.

As Pérez's trial began in early 1994, another massive scandal shook Venezuelan society with the collapse of the Banco Latino. According to the investigating judge, the bank which enjoyed political protection during the Pérez administration, was used to commit massive fraud with funds deposited by the public, companies, pension funds and even the government. Arrest warrants were issued for 83 people, including high-ranking shareholders and executives, allegedly responsible for the disappearance of hundreds of millions of dollars.

groups are concerned that the government's offshore 'Cristóbal Colón' gas project will seriously damage the environment around the Paria Peninsula. There are also concerns about extensive coal mining operations in Zulia State which are threatening indigenous communities, and the ecological impact of the mercury used in the Amazon by gold-seeking *garimpeiros*.

Drugs

The weekly death toll of young gang members is the most visible evidence of Venezuela's drugs industry. The *barrio* killings are caused by rising cocaine and *basuco* (a cheap cocaine derivative) consumption in poor areas and the struggle for control of the trade.

But the real money to be made from the international drug industry is not to be found in the *barrios* but among the higher echelons of Venezuelan society. The country does not produce cocaine, but acts as a transshipment point for the drug to reach the US or Europe from the Andean countries of Colombia and Peru. The recent discovery of 1,500 kg of cocaine in the British port of Felixstowe, hidden among a consignment of lead ingots, confirmed allegations of Venezuelan involvement in smuggling. There is also much evidence that military personnel are implicated in allowing cocaine to cross the border from Colombia and to reach Europe and the US.

Money laundering is another lucrative drug-related activity. In 1993, Venezuela's ambassador in Canada estimated that half of Latin America's illicit drug money was passing through Venezuelan banks *en route* to the US. This followed the arrest in 1992 of three Italian mafia members in a US$500 million money laundering scandal.

■ Human rights

National and international organisations claim that Venezuela is suffering an epidemic of human rights violations. In a November 1993 report, Amnesty International detailed many examples of torture, miscarriages of justice and extrajudicial executions. It claimed that political activists and students were prime targets and that poor inhabitants of the Caracas *barrios* are routinely arrested, tortured and even murdered by the security forces. In a cycle of violence, the so-called *malandros* (young criminals) kill and are killed, while many innocent slum dwellers are victimised because of where they live.

The main perpetrators of human rights violations, claims Amnesty, are the Metropolitan Police, the State Police and the undercover Directorate of Intelligence and Prevention Services (DISIP). These agencies, together with military groups, have been responsible for numerous illegal incidents especially after periods of social unrest. The riots of February 1989 and the two coup attempts of 1992 were followed by mass arrests and killings. In November 1990, after months of campaigning, relatives finally gained permission for the exhumation of bodies buried in a mass grave in Caracas. The exhumation revealed 68 corpses, most of them young males, which had been dumped in the cemetery after the 1989 riots.

Prison violence

The most disturbing aspect of Venezuela's human rights crisis has been a series of riots and mass killings in the country's prisons. The prison system is under enormous pressure, with overcrowding, corruption and staff morale at critical levels. Violent protests by inmates have been met with further violence from security forces, and since 1991 there have been deaths in several prisons.

In January 1994 a full-scale massacre occurred at a prison in Maracaibo when rival gangs fought with Molotov cocktails and guns before the riot was crushed by units of the National Guard. In the aftermath of the violence which cost 106 lives, the authorities admitted that the country's prisons held 30,000 inmates rather than the 14,000 maximum they were built to house.

■ Popular protest

With its history of dictatorship and two-party dominance, Venezuela does not have a tradition of political pluralism nor well established social movements. The two main parties have always tended to control and co-opt independent grassroots organisations and to turn them into electoral machines. Acción Democrática, in particular, has succeeded in maintaining a tight grip on the country's main trade union and peasant federations and in buying the support of neighbourhood organisations with promises of improved services and jobs.

Yet despite the all-pervasive influence of *partidocrácia,* some independent organisations have succeeded in registering protest at government policy and offering an alternative version of democratic participation. During the 1970s and 1980s, for instance, a number of neighbourhood associations sprang up in response to developers building on marginal land in Caracas and other cities. Their demands for ownership deeds and better services were supported by local church activists and other community groups.

Social movements have also made an impact over the environment and human rights. Successful protests have been mounted against oil and coal extraction in different parts of the country, and the government has been forced to take measures to protect Venezuela's extensive national parks. At the same time, groups such as PROVEA, Venezuela's national human rights monitoring organisation, have done much to expose and condemn instances of illegal arrest, torture and killings by the security forces. PROVEA's annual report is an invaluable analysis of all aspects of human rights in Venezuela. Indigenous groups, too, have made considerable progress in recent years in forming independent campaigning organisations.

The Church

From being one of the least progressive in Latin America, the Catholic Church has become an increasingly powerful force for social justice. Pope John Paul II criticised the Venezuelan hierarchy during his 1985 visit for lacking a vision of social change, and the Church has traditionally supported the government, receiving a large part of its funds from the state. For many years, it was largely irrelevant to most Venezuelans except in its Andean stronghold, and its political power was small by Latin American standards. But today in the shanty towns of all Venezuela's cities there are priests and lay workers, Venezuelan and foreign, who work with the poorest communities in education, health and different forms of self-help.

The Church has also become an important influence at a national level, criticising human rights abuses and mediating in political and social conflicts. The February 1989 'anti-IMF' riots were a turning point in this respect, and the Archbishop of Caracas made a controversial gesture by saying mass at the cemetery where the bodies of the 'disappeared' were exhumed. Since then, bishops have appeared regularly on television and in the press appealing for an end to state-sanctioned violence.

Women

In Venezuela, and particularly Caracas, women make up a large percentage of the middle-class, professional workforce. Women feature prominently in the legal profession, the media, medicine and engineering. Between 1970 and 1980 the number of women in the workforce doubled and this trend has continued since. In politics, however, women remain seriously under-represented, and the party bosses of both AD and COPEI are overwhelmingly men.

The growth of neighbourhood associations in the 1980s pushed many working-class women into positions of leadership. Many of the issues confronted by these organisations, such as food prices, health and education provision, were directly related to women's everyday experience as mothers and heads of household. The human rights situation in the *barrios* has been another focus for protest and organisation.

Yet a huge gulf separates Venezuela's middle-class female workforce from the poor of the shanty towns. Most middle-class families employ at least one woman domestic worker as cook, cleaner and childminder, and exploitation of these women is commonplace. The most vulnerable are Colombian immigrants, legal or illegal, who live under the constant threat of harassment or expulsion. More and more women now find that their employment opportunities are limited to the informal sector or low-paid service jobs such as shop assistants.

Venezuela's unusually liberal social legislation is a mixed blessing for many women. Although technically illegal, abortion is widely practised (an estimated 400,000 illegal abortions in 1993) and contraception is freely available. Divorce was legalised as early as 1909 and is a common phenomenon in Venezuelan society. Many middle-aged Venezuelans are in their second or even third marriage, and significant numbers of divorced women, unable to rely on alimony payments, are forced to go out to work.

Trade unions

Since it took its present-day form in the 1940s, the Confederation of Venezuelan Workers (CTV) has been run by the AD party. In the 1960s and

1970s the union was funded directly by the state, and now also has its own investments and business interests. Corruption is rife in the CTV, especially since its leaders have frequently accepted large bribes in return for ensuring that strikes do not take place. Venezuela's extraordinarily bureaucratic labour laws also make industrial action extremely difficult.

There are signs, however, that the CTV's stranglehold on Venezuelan labour is fading. A wave of strikes and protests by workers in health and education shook the Pérez government after the 1989 economic reform programme. As the government's commitment to the state sector has diminished and privatisations have gone ahead, so the CTV has lost many of its traditional strongholds. With the non-unionised informal and contract sector growing, the union is fast losing members and influence.

The old CTV bureaucracy has faced its biggest challenge, however, in the heavy industry sector of Guayana. Here, in the giant steel and aluminium plants the old traditions of co-option and repression have given way to a 'new unionism'. The struggle for control of the union at the SIDOR steel works goes back to the 1970s, when non-AD activists successfully won elections to the local leadership. Among them was Andrés Velásquez, an electrician, who has since become a leading political personality and governor of Bolívar State. Velásquez was fired and many other militants victimised or bought off, but despite a concerted campaign by the CTV old guard, the radical unionists retained their popularity and continue to dominate Ciudad Guayana.

Out of the SIDOR struggle emerged Causa R, the radical, trade union-based party which has shaken the political establishment since its first election victory in 1989. It is perhaps too early to judge whether Causa R, with its blend of anti-corruption campaigning and popular participation, will make further advances in Venezuelan politics. But its success so far is certainly a sign of the desire among many Venezuelans for fundamental political and social change.

5 CULTURE AND IDENTITY

Modern and Traditional

Forty kilometres out of the Andean city of Mérida, up a spectacular and winding mountain road, lies the village of Jají. With its charming central plaza, whitewashed buildings and craft shops, it is a major tourist attraction, and on Sundays coachloads of Venezuelans descend on the village to buy souvenirs. Nearby, the community of Los Aleros offers visitors the chance to ride in vintage cars and to relive daily life in a 1930s Andean village.

These sanitised versions of Andean life were constructed with government funding in the 1970s. Like the European or US 'heritage' industry, they present an idealised, comforting version of real history, where hardship and conflict are miraculously banished. They also reveal a nostalgic longing for some golden age of rural innocence, for how Venezuela might once have been.

Dominated much more by poverty than innocence, Venezuela's rural society disappeared in the decades following the discovery of oil. The dictatorships of Gómez and Pérez Jiménez saw intense social and demographic change. As Venezuela became an overwhelmingly urban nation, so people were uprooted from villages and farms to be transplanted in the tower blocks and suburbs of the cities.

The cities themselves were entirely reconstructed. Little remains today of Caracas' once famous pastel-coloured colonial houses and elegant gardens, even less of the sugar-cane and coffee which used to grow in the valley. Many slums were bulldozed in the process, but so too were traditional working-class neighbourhoods and old colonial quarters, to be replaced by modern apartment blocks, motorways and enormous skyscrapers.

Concrete jungle

Caracas can seem like a parody of urban modernity. Wherever possible, buildings are on a massive scale. The Parque Central complex, built between 1970 and 1986, boasts 56-storey blocks housing government offices and museums. The two main arterial roads which dissect the city have been lifted above street level on a series of flyovers. To the east, the CCCT shopping centre is one of the biggest in the Americas. Advertisements are everywhere; the names of transnationals gleam in neon from office skyscrapers. Even the slums which line the road to the airport huddle under giant hoardings devoted to Fuji film and Marlboro.

■ **US influences**

The influence of North American lifestyles and culture is undeniable. Since oil broke Venezuela's cycle of rural poverty, the US has been a constant presence in the country. The prospectors and companies which rushed to take advantage of oil concessions in the 1920s and 1930s were followed by other firms, eager to do business with oil-rich Venezuela. North American consumer tastes and habits began to replace more traditional European cultural influences as wealthy Venezuelans turned to the US for their shopping trips and children's education. The 'Americanisation' of Venezuela accelerated in the 1960s and 1970s with the return of formal democracy and the influx of petro-dollars.

Today, North American influence takes many forms. On a superficial level, the Venezuelan obsession with beauty contests (an impressive number of Venezuelan women have won the Miss World and Miss Universe contests) is widely seen as a US import. Revealingly, the most successful *Misses* are rarely anything other than pale-skinned and blond. The car culture and advent of drive-in, fast-food consumerism also bear the US hallmark.

Sport

Venezuela is the only country in South America where football is not the national game. Although the sport has a following in the Andean region, the real passion for most Venezuelans is baseball. In its sporting tastes (which also include basketball and boxing), Venezuela has more in common with Central American and Caribbean countries such as Nicaragua, Cuba and the Dominican Republic than with its immediate neighbours.

Baseball came to the country with the advent of oil and the arrival of US oil workers. It was first played in the oil workers' camps but soon spread around the country. Today, there is a professional baseball league of eight clubs, which attract huge crowds and fanatical support. The traditional needle match is between the clubs from Caracas and Valencia.

Baseball is played in every village, school and shanty town in Venezuela. The fashion accessories of caps and club shirts are almost universal, and national television serves up a constant diet of the game. For some poor Venezuelans, the game offers a way out of obscurity and a passport to international success. Many Venezuelans, particularly blacks, have made it into the US *grandes ligas,* while some North Americans come to Venezuela to play in the winter league.

Television

US cultural influence is perhaps most pervasive in Venezuela's mass media. The country has the highest per capita access to television in Latin America, and even the worst shanty towns in Caracas sprout a forest of TV aerials.

Sport, one possible escape
from the *barrio*.
(Ricardo Bravo)

The mass media in Venezuela is concentrated into extremely powerful private companies such as the Cisneros group which controls TV channels, recording studios, radio stations, computer companies and video distribution. These companies, as well as the government-run media, depend heavily on US corporations for programmes, technology and investment.

The arrival of CNN, satellite television and home video viewing has further deepened the impact of the US media. In 1991, studies revealed that almost 60 per cent of Venezuelan television's programming was imported, mostly from North America. Advertising accounts for almost 10 per cent of broadcasting time and much of it is for US goods and services. While Venezuelan television tends to produce its own news and current affairs programmes, the much more popular films and serials are imported.

Soap operas

Television is not entirely a one-way trade. The *telenovela* or soap opera may have originated in the US, but Venezuela has taken it over and made it its own. The genre has its own rules and conventions: improbably glamorous stars, completely implausible plots and totally unbelievable conclusions. The formula seems to work, not only in Venezuela. Soaps from Caracas are exported to Argentina, Chile, Mexico, Spain, Italy and to the growing Hispanic networks in the US.

Telenovelas usually dramatise the lives of the rich and beautiful. But some Venezuelan soaps have taken more ambitious political and historical themes and offer a limited amount of social commentary. The life of Simón Bolívar, for instance, formed the basis for a long-running serial, while the Gómez dictatorship was the unlikely subject for a popular melodrama. Others have touched on issues of poverty, violence and human rights abuses in the *barrios*.

■ **Pop culture**

The thriving soap opera industry is part of a broader commercial network which encompasses music, cinema and publishing. Many soap opera stars are also singers, and their CDs or cassettes are often marketed by the same media conglomerates which broadcast the soaps. Caracas is an international centre for *salsa* and boasts world-class recording facilities as well as a vibrant nightclub circuit. Musicians from Puerto Rico, the Dominican Republic and Central America are drawn to Caracas, where fortunes can still be made.

Oscar d'León, a one time taxi-driver and car-worker, is Venezuela's top international *salsero*. Since the 1970s, his bands have had countless hits, and d'León who sings, dances and plays bass, has become a national institution. There are many imitators of his big-band style, including his former group *La Dimensión Latina,* and *salsa* bands regularly tour even the furthest flung regions of Venezuela.

The world of soap operas, *salsa* and beauty queens has created the phenomenon of *farándula* (the word means something like claptrap or con-trick), the hype and gossip which surround the lives of Venezuelan stars. Glossy magazines and television chatshows follow every movement of celebrities such as 'el Puma', and sensationalism and scandal are essential ingredients. To outsiders *farándula* may appear trivial; to its followers it is the stuff of life.

Caracas has more to offer culturally than soap operas. Oil bonanzas over the years have enabled governments to invest in orchestras, theatres, art galleries and museums, and Caracas has an impressive range of classic paintings and sculptures including work by El Greco, Picasso and Henry Moore. Many of Venezuela's leading artists have contributed work to the

Caracas Metro, where sculptures, murals and stained glass decorate many of the stations. The kinetic sculptor, Jesús Soto, is perhaps the best-known local artist, and his home city of Ciudad Bolívar has a museum of his work. Venezuelan cinema is also thriving, despite the economic crisis and cutbacks in state support. Like much other Latin America cinema, it tends to concentrate on social and political themes, often with a strong concern for human rights. Carlos Azpúrua's *Disparen a matar* (Shoot to Kill), made in 1991, deals with a police killing of an innocent man in a Caracas *barrio* and his mother's attempt to break through an official cover-up. Another recurring concern with Venezuelan film-makers is the history and present-day plight of the country's indigenous population.

■ Music and fiestas

Symphony orchestras and *salsa* apart, Venezuela has a rich repertoire of traditional and folk music. Perhaps the best-known rhythm is the *joropo,* an energetic dance for couples which features accordeon, harp, *cuatro* (a small four-stringed guitar) and *maracas.* Different regions have different versions of the *joropo,* and the dance invariably features in local festivals and feast days.

Carnival is Venezuela's main national festival, but every region has its own variation on the basic recipe of religion, rum and music. In the more conservative and traditional Andes, the fusion of indigenous and Catholic beliefs takes the form of village *fiestas patronales* (saint's day festivals), where processions and church services precede the festivities. In San Francisco de Yare, the mood is altogether more burlesque as dancers dressed as devils compete for the most grotesque costume. The Corpus Christi devil dancing ritual was perhaps once intended to ward off evil, but now it is a major tourist attraction and pretext for merrymaking.

The most exuberant *fiesta* takes place in July in the coastal area of Barlovento, traditionally the centre of Afro-Venezuela and the region of former plantations. The three-day *Fiesta de San Juan,* in honour of St John the Baptist, features the rhythmic music of the *tambores,* huge hollow logs used as drums. After a good deal of rum and dancing, statues of St John are paraded around villages and occasionally baptised in rivers.

Popular religions

Although nominally a Catholic nation, Venezuela is probably the least devout country in Latin America. A small percentage of Venezuelans are regular church-goers, and the Church does not exert the same influence as in neighbouring states. Protest evangelical sects are also much less important in Venezuela than elsewhere in the region. With its mix of indigenous, African and European influences, however, Venezuela has some distinctive popular religious beliefs which attract large numbers of followers. Some of

Icons of Dr José Gregorio
Hernández, doctor of the poor
and popular saint.
(Fundación Bigott)

these revolve around historical figures such as Simón Bolívar, whose effigy is widely venerated as a source of supernatural power and assistance.

One of the most popular spiritual icons is Dr José Gregorio Hernández, a medical doctor who died in 1918 after a career helping the poor of the Andes and then Caracas. His effigy appears in many forms, always wearing hat, suit and tie and carrying his doctor's bag. It is believed that Dr Hernández's cures were often miraculous and that his intervention can still help to banish illness and unhappiness. The Catholic Church has taken this massive devotion seriously and is considering Dr Hernández for canonisation as a saint.

The cult of María Lionza, on the other hand, is unlikely to win the Vatican's approval. This popular synthesis of catholicism, African beliefs and indigenous mythology has many followers from all classes and regions who believe that they can make contact with María Lionza through a state of trance or possession by other spirits. Like voodoo, the spirit's powers can be used for good or evil, and believers can endure intense pain when in their trance-like state. The actual identity of María Lionza herself remains a mystery, although effigies of a pale-skinned crowned young woman are to be seen throughout Venezuela.

■ Regional identity

Partly Caribbean, partly Andean and partly *llanero,* Venezuela has a mixed identity to match the varied origins of its inhabitants. If the advent of TV culture and modern communications has created an urbanised, US-

The Call of the llanos

Most middle-class urban Venezuelans tend to wax lyrical over the wild and desolate *llanos*, the frontier territory so far removed from cosmopolitan Caracas. The rough *llanero* is the Venezuelan equivalent of the Argentinian *gaucho*, a romantic and mysterious cowboy-figure, whose freedom and proximity to nature stand in contrast to most modern, sedentary lifestyles. The best-known example of the *llanos* cult is *Doña Bárbara*, a novel published in 1929 by Rómulo Gallegos and now approaching its fiftieth edition. Gallegos (1884-1969) was a founder member of Acción Democrática and was President during the 1945-8 *trienio*. He wrote his most famous novel in exile in Europe during the Gómez dictatorship, but it has lost little of its appeal to today's Venezuelan readers. Its importance lies in the way that it moves beyond merely imitating contemporary European themes and style to create a new, specifically South American vision of a country undergoing social transformation.

The story concerns the struggle between Doña Bárbara, a woman who epitomises the elemental forces of the *llanos* and Santos Luzardo, the cultured *Caraqueño*, who symbolises the advance of modernity into the frontier wilderness. Eventually, Santos Luzardo triumphs over Doña Bárbara by marrying her daughter, Marisela, confirming the victory of civilisation over nature. Yet although Gallegos concludes with an image of the *llanos* tamed by railway lines and barbed wire fences, the mystique of the open plains remains intact. The novel ends with the narrator's lyrical vision of the region as a 'landscape of open horizons where a fine race loves, suffers and hopes'.

influenced society, old regional traditions and identities persist. People from Mérida and San Cristóbal, for instance, pride themselves on being different from *Caraqueños*, more reserved, formal and serious about life. The inhabitants of Maracaibo, on the other hand, have a reputation for brashness and ostentation, as befits the oil-producing Texas of Venezuela. The sparsely inhabited *llanos*, meanwhile, maintain their romantic aura of a frontier territory, with simple and unsophisticated customs.

Venezuela's mixed regional identity is reflected in relations with neighbouring countries. During the oil boom years Venezuela had ambitions to become a regional power, asserting its economic and political authority as an alternative to both US dominance and the Cuban model of socialism. President Pérez, in particular, saw himself as a prominent Third World leader, and Venezuela took the initiative in various aid and cooperation schemes. During the 1970s and 1980s, it gave aid and assistance to small Caribbean states such as Grenada, while Pérez maintained close relations with Jamaica's social-democratic Prime Minister, Michael Manley. Pérez also lent his support to the Contadora Group of Latin American nations which was seeking a peaceful solution to the civil wars in Central America.

The second Pérez administration continued to intervene in the Caribbean, most notably supporting the ousted Haitian president, Jean-Bertrand Aristide, in his struggle against Haiti's military dictatorship. But policy towards Nicaragua changed, as Venezuela backed the UNO opposition which defeated the Sandinistas in February 1990's elections. Policy towards Cuba remains an ambiguous mix of symbolic support for the communist regime (such as inviting Fidel Castro to Pérez's inauguration) and pragmatic neutrality.

Sometimes Venezuela's mixed diplomatic objectives can create contradictions and difficulties. During the post-1992 Single European Market dispute over banana exports to Europe, Venezuela has sided with Latin American producers such as Costa Rica in their attempt to increase access to European markets. This has incurred the wrath of Caribbean producers, especially those in the Windward Islands, who depend on protected market access. Equally, Venezuela's high-profile activities within OPEC have not always been appreciated by neighbouring Trinidad, which is not an OPEC member.

■ Good Neighbour?

Venezuela's main foreign policy problems lie in its relations with its immediate neighbours, Brazil, Guyana and Colombia. Each of these countries has had territorial disputes with Venezuela, and even today there is considerable tension with Colombia.

The problem with Brazil surrounds the remote and ill-defined frontier in the Amazon region, where *garimpeiros* are invading indigenous land and occasionally clashing with communities on Venezuelan territory. Venezuela has a longer-standing border dispute with Guyana over the Essequibo region which it claims as its own territory. This dispute dates back to the 17th century, when Spain ceded present-day Guyana to Holland without determining clear borders. After centuries of arguments and inconclusive arbitration, the issue is not yet resolved, even if relations between Caracas and Georgetown are relatively cordial.

The conflict between Venezuela and Colombia is altogether more serious. The territorial issue at stake is the Gulf of Venezuela, the waters which join Lake Maracaibo to the Caribbean, and control over this vital conduit for Venezuela's oil exports. Border clashes have taken place, and in 1988 a Colombian warship provocatively sailed into Venezuelan waters, sparking off talks of armed conflict.

But a deeper antagonism underlines these border incidents. Many Venezuelans regard Colombians as illegal immigrants, cheap labour and criminals. Drug-trafficking over the border has become widespread, undoubtedly with local police connivance, and there have been occasional shoot-outs between Venezuelan military patrols and alleged Colombian guerrillas. One such incident in October 1988 prompted reports that Venezuelan military and DISIP units had killed 16 guerrillas who were crossing the border in order to kidnap Venezuelan landowners. Only later did it become clear that the guerrillas were in fact unarmed Venezuelan fishermen. A proper explanation for this massacre has so far been withheld. At the same time, politicians on both sides of the border are only too willing to stir up xenophobic passions against the neighbouring country for their own ends.

Whether Venezuela's strained relationship with Colombia improves through increased trade remains to be seen. But for as long as its economic woes persist, Venezuela's ambition to be a regional power seems likely to remain just an ambition.

CONCLUSION

All good things must come to an end. For Venezuela the halcyon days of oil wealth are finished, at least for the time being, and the country must face the prospect of a difficult economic future. Venezuelans have already tasted structural adjustment and austerity and rejected them overwhelmingly. In the end, the *gran viraje* ground to a halt, as corruption, popular opposition and the threat of military intervention stalled the reform programme.

Rafael Caldera inherited a nation in crisis. Economically precarious, politically volatile and socially explosive, Venezuela seemed nostalgic for the past, unwilling to accept its fall from grace. A political power vacuum developed as the old system of patronage and power-sharing unravelled. With his message of clean government and prioritising the poor, Caldera struck a popular chord. His aim, he said, was to end the country's 'free-market misery'.

But the promise may be hard to deliver. Caldera is obstructed by a hostile Congress and limited by a chronic shortfall in government income. The collapse of several national banks has forced the government to intervene at great expense. Food and transport riots again shook Caracas in mid-1994. The *bolívar* continues to drop in value, and Caldera rules by decree.

Perhaps the worst is already past. Further military unrest is not generally considered an immediate threat, especially as Caldera has wisely raised wages for the armed forces and pardoned many of the ringleaders of the 1992 coups. The economy may improve if political stability returns and investment resumes. Growing integration with Latin American and Caribbean neighbours may also allow Venezuela to diversify its trading partners and expand its range of non-petroleum exports.

Ultimately, however, Venezuela's economic future remains firmly tied to the future of the international oil industry. With its large deposits of heavy and 'dirty' crudes, the country faces an uphill struggle in an ecologically sensitive world market, especially in the US. On the other hand, its investments in refining and distribution around the world have given Venezuela a solid stake in the industry's future. As with all commodities, that future can never be certain. All that is predictable about Venezuela's future is that further political and social change is inevitable. Whether this change is peaceful or violent will depend on whether economic redistribution takes place. Without reform another *caracazo* cannot be long in coming.

FURTHER READING AND ADDRESSES

Amnesty International, *Venezuela: the Eclipse of Human Rights*. London, 1993.

Boué, J.C., *Venezuela: The Political Economy of Oil*. Oxford, 1993.

Dunsterville Branch, H., *Venezuela*. Chalfont St Peter, 1993.

Ellner, S., 'The Venezuelan Left: From Years of Prosperity to Economic Crisis.' In Carr, B and S. Ellner, *The Latin American Left*. London, 1993.

Galeano, E., *Open Veins of Latin America*. New York, 1974.

Hellinger, D.C., *Venezuela: Tarnished Democracy*. Boulder, CO, 1991.

Insight Guides, *Venezuela*. Hong Kong, 1992.

Levine, D.H., *Conflict and Political Change in Venezuela*. Princeton, 1973.

Lombardi, J., *Venezuela: The Search for Order, the Dream of Progress*. New York, 1982.

Martz, J.D., 'Party Elites and Leadership in Colombia and Venezuela.' In *Journal of Latin American Studies,* vol. 24, 1, 1992.

Michelena, S. (ed.), *Venezuela hacia el 2000: desafíos y opciones*. Caracas, 1991.

NACLA, *Report on the Americas, 'Venezuela: Rethinking Capitalist Democracy.'* New York, 1994.

Naím, M. and R. Piñango (eds.), *El caso Venezuela*. Caracas, 1985.

Philip, G., *Oil and Politics in Latin America: Nationalist Movements and State Companies*. Cambridge, 1982.

PROVEA, *Situación de los derechos humanos en Venezuela: informe anual, septiembre 1992-octubre 1993*. Caracas, 1993.

Randall, L., *The Political Economy of Venezuelan Oil*. New York, 1987.

Tulchin, J.S. (ed.), *Venezuela in the Wake of Radical Reform*. Boulder, CO, 1993.

Wright, W.R., *Café con leche: Race, Class and National Image in Venezuela*. Austin, 1990.

One of the best sources of news and analysis on Venezuela is the Jesuit monthly magazine, *Sic,* published by the Centro Gumilla, Edificio Centro Valores, local 2, Esquina de la Luneta, Apartado 4838, Caracas 1010-A, Venezuela.

ADDRESSES

Venezuelan Embassy (Consular Section),
56 Grafton Way,
London W1P 5LB
Tel. 071-387-6727
(information pack available)

Journey Latin America,
14-16 Devonshire Road,
London W4 2HD
Tel. 081-747-3108
(specialist travel agents)

Last Frontiers Ltd,
Swan House, High Street,
Long Crendon,
Buckinghamshire HP18 9AF
Tel. 0844-208405
(specialising in tours to Venezuela)

Geodyssey,
29 Harberton Road,
London N19 3JS
Tel. 071-281-7788
(small group journeys to Venezuela)

Cooperation for Development,
118 Broad Street
Chesham,
Buckinghamshire HP5 3ED
Tel. 0494-775557
(development agency with programme in Venezuela)

British Embassy and Consulate,
Torre Las Mercedes, 3rd Floor,
Av. La Estancia, Chuao, Caracas
Tel. 751-1022

FACTS AND FIGURES

See also reference map

A   GEOGRAPHY

Official name: República de Venezuela (YV, VEN)
Situation: in northern South America, between 12°11' and 0°45' N and 59°45' and 73°11' W. Maximum east-west distance c. 1500 km; north-south 1300 km.
Surface area: 912,050 sq km (3.7 x UK; 1.3 x Texas).
Administrative division: Venezuela is a federal republic, comprising 22 *estados* (states), one federal district (Caracas), and 72 federal dependencies (the small offshore islands).
Capital: Caracas, 1,824,892 inhabitants (1991); over 4 million inhabitants (1994, including suburbs)
Other cities (1991 census): Maracaibo (1.37 million) Valencia (1.03 million), Maracay (957,000), Barquisimeto (787,000), Ciudad Guayana (543,000), Barcelona/ Puerto la Cruz (455,000), San Cristóbal (365,000), Ciudad Bolívar (286,000), Maturín (277,000), Mérida (275,000), Cumaná (270,000).
Infrastructure: well-developed road network, 77,500 km of which 26,300 km paved; major roads link Caracas with Ciudad Bolívar, Colombia (the Pan-American Highway) and Brazil; the railway network at present only covers the 268 km line from Barquisimeto to Puerto Cabello and two freight lines near Ciudad Guayana. There are plans to extend it to 2,000 km

Time difference
London 12.00 noon
Caracas 8.00 a.m.
Washington D.C. 7.00 a.m.

by the year 2005; Caracas has a metro system (opened 1983); international airport at Caracas, there is also a network of 61 airports throughout the country; national airline VIASA (60% owned by *Iberia);* domestic flights by *Avensa* (private) and *Aeropostal* (state-run, up for sale); principal ports are La Guiara, Puerto Cabello and Maracaibo, there are also 17 oil shipping terminals.
Relief and landscape: Venezuela's varied landscapes can be divided into four principal areas: the coast and coastal highlands, the Andes, the *llanos* or plains and the Guayana Highlands. The coast includes the Maracaibo basin, with its large but shallow semi-salt lake (12,800 sq km), the highlands of Caracas (960 m), Maracay (445 m) and Valencia (480 m), where mountains rise from the coast to a height of up

to 3,000 m, the Barlovento area between Caracas and Barcelona, the state of Sucre (Paria and Araya peninsulas), and the Orinoco delta. Offshore are the Venezuelan Caribbean islands. Most Venezuelan agriculture is based in the semi-tropical coastal zones, and most oil and industrial production in the large cities. The Andes run from the coastal range into the 500 km-long Sierra Nevada de Mérida range. The five highest peaks exceed 4,500 m, but most people live in valleys between 800 m and 1,300 m. The highest peak is Pico Bolívar at 5,007 m. The *llanos,* mostly flat grasslands and slow running rivers, cover 30% of the country's area but are sparsely populated (10% of total population). Slight hillocks or *mesas* rise to a maximum of 250 m. Heavy rains from April to October cause the region to flood, but

VENEZUELA

States and State Capitals

D.F.   Distrito Federal (Federal District)
Dep. Fed. Dependencias Federales (Federal
           Dependent Territories) Tortuga and
           71 other small Caribbean islands

1 San Felipe
2 Valencia
3 Maracay

VENEZUELA

Climate Areas

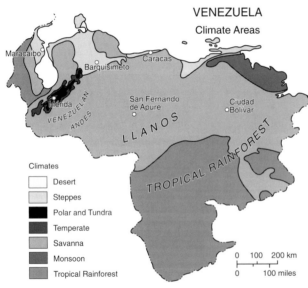

Climates

☐	Desert
☐	Steppes
■	Polar and Tundra
■	Temperate
■	Savanna
■	Monsoon
■	Tropical Rainforest

est peak is Mt Roraima at 2,810 m. Remarkable is the 979 m high Angel Falls in the Gran Sabana area, the highest in the world. Large parts of Amazonas are covered with tropical rainforest. The Casiquiare River is a natural connection between the Orinoco and Amazone river basins.

Temperature and rainfall: Venezuela is a tropical country but the influence of mountains, sea and trade winds gives a great variety in rainfall, temperatures and climate areas (see map). Most of the country has a dry season from December to April. Mean temperatures vary from Mérida (19°C/66°F) to Ciudad Bolívar (29°C/84°F). Caracas has a moderate climate (20°C/68°F), but can be quite cold at night. Average rainfall also varies, from the dry desert and steppe areas around Maracaibo (570 mm per year) to over 2,500 mm in the rainforests of Amazonas state. The north-eastern trade winds give the mangrove-covered Orinoco delta a monsoon climate.

Flora and fauna: Venezuela's diversity of rainfall, altitude and temperature produces a wide variety of plant and animal life. The humid tropical zones produce cacao, bananas, coconuts, mangoes, palm and rubber trees, while cacti and prickly pears grow in the dry areas. The semi-tropical regions (500-1,000 m) produce oranges, lemons, avocados, tobacco, sugar-cane, cotton and rice. The temperate zones (above 1,000 m) produce coffee, maize, beans and potatoes. There is a vast spectrum of animal life, especially in the Amazon region. The rain forest contains jaguars, different types of monkey, anteaters, tapirs, crocodiles, alligators and numerous varieties of birds, fish and insect life.

between November and March drought forces the region's livestock towards the Orinoco. The Guayana Highlands cover 45% of the country's area and lie to the south of the Orinoco. They rise, in forested hills and valleys to flat-topped tablelands on the border with Brazil. A mixture of savannas and semi-deciduous forests, the region is very sparsely populated (5% of total) with the exception of the new industrial conurbations of Ciudad Guayana and Ciudad Bolívar, where 87% of the population lives. The high-

B

POPULATION

Population (1994): 20.7 million
(census 1991: 18,105,265).
Population growth: 1965-80:
4.8%, 1980-92: 2.6%.
Population density (1994):
23 inhabitants per sq km.
Urbanisation: 91%.
Age structure: 0-14: 37%, 14-64:
61%, 65+: 2%.
Fertility (1992): an average Ven-
ezuelan woman has 3.6 children.
Birthrate (1992): 30 per 1,000.
Mortality rate (1992): 5 per 1,000.
Infant mortality (1992): 35 per
1,000.
Average life expectancy (1992):
men: 67, women: 73.
Population per doctor: 590
(1989), 1,210 (1965).
Per capita calorie consumption:
2,547 (104% of required intake).
Adult illiteracy (1992): 11%.
Education: primary education is
free and compulsory between the
ages of 7 and 13; secondary education lasts a further six years.
According to UN estimates, only
50% of children complete their
basic education.
Universities: 11 state universities, 13 private universities,
106 higher education institutes.
*Social Development Index (UNDP
Human Development Index 1992):*
44th out of 47 in high group (UK
10th, US 6th), total 160 positions.
Ethnic composition: 69% *mestizo*
(mixed Indian-European descent),
20% European, 9% African, 2%
indigenous Indian.
Language: Spanish; 21 distinct

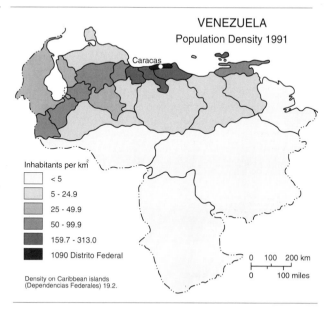

VENEZUELA
Population Density 1991

Inhabitants per km²

- □ < 5
- □ 5 - 24.9
- ▨ 25 - 49.9
- ▨ 50 - 99.9
- ▩ 159.7 - 313.0
- ■ 1090 Distrito Federal

Density on Caribbean islands
(Dependencias Federales) 19.2.

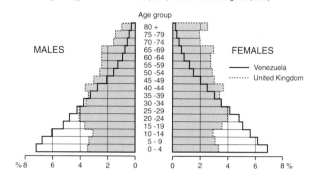

Age-sex pyramids of Venezuela (1991) and the United Kingdom (1989)

Age group

MALES   FEMALES

———— Venezuela
········· United Kingdom

indigenous languages are also
spoken.
Religion: mostly Roman Cath-

olic, also several 'popular cults',
some evangelical protestant
churches.

SOURCES

World Bank; IMF; UNDP; Overseas
Development Administration;
Petróleos de Venezuela S.A.;

Europa Publications, *South
America, Central America and
the Caribbean 1993;* Economist

Intelligence Unit, *Latin America
Monitor,* London.

C   HISTORY AND POLITICS

Some key dates • 1498: Christopher Columbus arrives in Gulf of Paria • 1499: Alonso de Ojeda's expedition gives the name Venezuela • 1528: Spain cedes Venezuela to German Welser banking house (Germans depart c. 20 years later) • 1567: Caracas founded • 1728: Basque *Compañía Guipuzcoana* takes trading monopoly (until c. 1780) • 1783: birth of Simón Bolívar • 1811: first independence movement against Spain • 1821: Spanish defeated at battle of Carabobo • 1830: death of Bolívar • after 1830-1888: 730 armed conflicts and 26 insurrections • 1854: abolition of slavery • 1859-63: Federal War between Liberals and Conservatives • 1908-35: dictatorship of Juan Vicente Gómez • 1922: first large discovery of oil • 1935: death of Gómez • 1941: Acción Democrática (AD) founded • 1945-48: *trienio* of AD rule • 1946: COPEI founded • 1948: military coup led by Marcos Pérez Jiménez • 1958: return of civilian rule and Pact of Punto Fijo • 1960: founding of OPEC • 1969-73: first Rafael Caldera government • 1973: beginning of 10-year oil boom • 1974-8: first administration of Carlos Andrés Pérez • 1976: nationalisation of oil industry • 1979-83 administra-

tion of Luís Herrera Campins • 1983: *bolívar* devalued, end of oil-boom • 1984-8: administration of Jaime Lusinchi • 1989-93: second Pérez administration • 27-2-1989: *caracazo* and austerity riots in 19 other cities • 1992: two attempted military coups put down by loyal troops • 1993: impeachment of President Pérez; interim presidency of Ramón José Velásquez; 5-12-93: election victory for Rafael Caldera • 2-2-94: start second administration Caldera • 1994: collapse of Banco Latino; Caldera enacts economic policy by decree.
Constitution: Presidential republic; the constitution of 1961 gives executive power to a president, elected for a 5-year term by universal suffrage. Legislative power is exercised by the *Senado* (50 seats) and *Cámara de diputados* (204 seats), also elected for 5 years by universal suffrage. Magistrates of the Supreme Court, the highest tribunal, are elected by both chambers in joint sessions. Voting is theoretically compulsory for all over 18.
Head of State: Rafael Caldera (since 2 February 1994).
Political parties (with seats in Cámara de diputados and Senado (1994): Acción Democrática (AD, Democratic Action), 58 and 16; Comité de Organiza-

ción Política Electoral Independiente (COPEI, Independent Electoral Political Organising Committee), 53 and 14; La Causa R (LCR, Radical Cause), 41 and 9; *Convergencia,* 26 and 6; Movimiento al Socialismo *(MAS,* Movement Towards Socialism), 26 and 5.
Military expenditure as % of combined education and health expenditure (1990-91): 33% (UK 40%, US 46%).
Armed forces (1990): 70,500 (48% army, 14% navy, 9% airforce, 29% National Guard) of whom 18,000 approx. are conscripts. Defence spending is 1.1% of GDP.
Membership of international organisations: UN and UN organisations, Organisation of American States (OAS), Andean Pact, Group of Three (G-3), Latin American Integration Association (LAIA), OPEC, IMF.
Media/communications: There are a total of 69 daily newspapers (1990), with several large-circulation papers published in Caracas *(El Diario, El Mundo, El Nacional, El Universal)* and many local papers in provincial cities; there are five major TV stations (as well as satellite and cable) and 185 radio stations nationally.

D   ECONOMY

Currency: bolívar (Bs); Bs = US$ 1989: 34.7, 1991: 56.8, 1993: 90.8, Feb. 1994: 107.3, 7 July 1994: 170.
Inflation: 1980-92: 23%, 1992: 31.9%, 1993: 46%, first 6 months

1994: 100%.
Gross Domestic Product (GDP): US$58.7 billion (1993).
Per capita GDP (1993): US$2,830.
Economic growth: 1970-80:

3.5%, 1980-92: 1.9%, 1989: -7.8%, 1990: 6.9%, 1991: 9.7%, 1992: 6.8%, 1993: -1.0%.
Foreign debt (1994): US$38 billion.
Debt servicing as % of exports

and services: 19.5% (1992).
Development aid (1991): US$1.7
per capita
GDP per sector (1992): agriculture 5%, manufacturing 16%,
mining 25%, services 53%.
Employment by sector (1991):
agriculture: 10.6%, oil and
mining: 0.9%, manufacturing:
15%, construction: 7.6%,
services: 57.1%.
Unemployment (1994): 7%;

informal sector 40%.
Exports: total value (1992/93)
US$14.0/14.2 billion; main
exports (1992): petroleum
(US$11.2bn, 79%), metals
(US$1.2bn, 9%), chemicals
(US$324m), cars and parts
(US$120m).
Imports: total value (1992/93):
US$12.2/10.7 billion; main
imports (1992): machinery
(US$3.8bn, 31%), transport

equipment (US$2.6bn, 21%),
chemicals (US$1.4bn), metals
(US$960m).
*Principal trading partners
(1992):* exports: US (50.8%),
Netherlands (7.8%), Germany
(4.4%), Japan (3.0%), Brazil
(2.2%), others (31.8%); imports:
US (47.7%), Germany (6.1%),
Japan (6.0%), Italy (4.7%),
Brazil (4.1%), others (31.4%).

E   VENEZUELA AND BRITAIN/UNITED STATES

Trade relations with Britain: In
1993 (up to September) the value
of Venezuelan exports to Britain
totalled £92 million. Main exports were petroleum products
(£57 million), metal ores (£13
million) and other raw materials
(£13 million). In the same period,
British exports to Venezuela
totalled £165 million, comprising
principally beverages (£59 million), chemicals (£20 million)
and power generating equipment
(£13 million).
Trade relations with the US: In
1992 the US was Venezuela's big-

gest trading partner for imports
and exports. Venezuelan exports
to the US totalled more than
US$7 billion, of which petroleum
and related products accounted
for more than 80%. The main
imports from the US were transport equipment, machinery,
chemicals and metals, totalling
approximately US$4 billion.
*Aid and development relations
with Britain:* Total official British aid to Venezuela in 1992/3
totalled £251,000. Because Venezuela has a relatively high per
capita GDP, it does not receive

much aid from governments or
from NGOs. The only British
agency with a programme in
Venezuela is Cooperation for
Development, which assists
small farmers and producers with
credit schemes.
*Aid and development relations
with the US:* The FY 1994 US overseas aid budget proposes US$1.5
million for Venezuela, of which
US$1 million is earmarked for
anti-narcotics activities. Few US
NGOs operate in Venezuela.

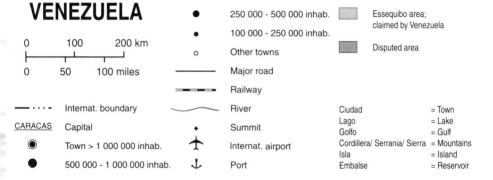

VENEZUELA

| 0 | 100 | 200 km |
| 0 | 50 | 100 miles |

● 250 000 - 500 000 inhab.
● 100 000 - 250 000 inhab.
○ Other towns
—— Major road
▬▬▬ Railway
〜 River
✦ Summit
✈ Internat. airport
⚓ Port

▓ Essequibo area;
claimed by Venezuela
▓ Disputed area

—···· Internat. boundary
CARACAS Capital
◎ Town > 1 000 000 inhab.
● 500 000 - 1 000 000 inhab.

Ciudad	= Town
Lago	= Lake
Golfo	= Gulf
Cordillera/ Serrania/ Sierra	= Mountains
Isla	= Island
Embalse	= Reservoir

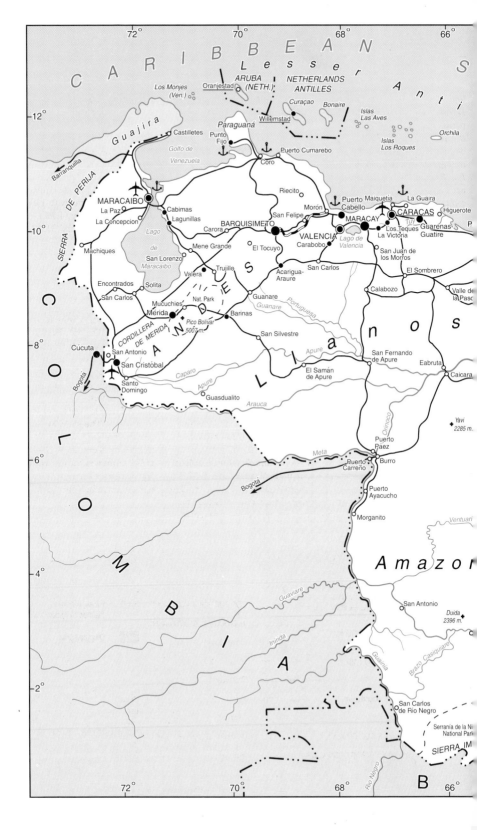